SATANIC SHADOWS

DEPICTIONS OF HELL & THE DEVIL IN EARLY CINEMA
AN ILLUSTRATED FILMOGRAPHY 1896–1936

SATANIC SHADOWS
ISBN 978-1-84068-695-1
Edited by G.H. Janus

Published in the USA by Deicide Press 2023
With special thanks to Black Gas Entertainment
Design: Broken Fang Cryptography

SATANIC SHADOWS

FOREWORD

Fictive narratives in primal cinema were mainly derived from the staging of magic tricks for the camera or the filmic recreation of iconic scenes from literature and legend. Bestriding and often uniting these twin tropes was the singular figure of Satan, the Devil, also known as Mephistopheles, Lucifer, and other mythic apellations. From Goethe's Faust to Dante's graphic renderings of the Inferno, classic art and literature were the well whence sprang the first cinematic depictions of the Devil and his dwelling-place.

From Georges Méliès' **Le Manoir Du Diable**, shot in 1896, through Milano's 1911 staging of **L'Inferno** and Benjamin Christensen's superlative **Häxan** of 1921 to ground-breaking animated cartoons of the mid-1930s, SATANIC SHADOWS documents all of the key filmic invocations of Satan, his victims and his worshippers unleashed in the first four decades of commercial cinema. Trick-films, slapstick comedies, morality tales, religious fables, phantasies of infernal terror, and even clandestine stag reels; all contain within their canon the cinematic spectre of Satan.

Comprising a comprehensive illustrated filmography of early satanic cinema and the roots of the horror genre, SATANIC SHADOWS shows how narratives of sin, temptation and damnation were central to these works, and how the Devil's dark, horned figure overshadowed all others in the race to astonish and terrify the spectator. The book references over 250 films, and also features a wide array of more than 100 illuminating production photographs, many assembled from numerous film archives and seldom, if ever, previously published.

ACKNOWLEDGEMENT
All text and graphic works in this book were selected, collated and edited under license from **Shadows In A Phantom Eye,** the ongoing multi-volume global film history from The Nocturne Group which is already, in my opinion, proving to be among the best of its kind ever published. The history of Satan in cinema is just one of the hundreds of intertwining threads contained in this seminal series.

–G.H. Janus, 2022

GUSTAVE DORÉ, *DANTE ET VERGIL DANS LE NEUVIÈME CERCLE DE L'ENFER* – PAINTING, 1861 (*DETAIL, OPPOSITE*).

LE MANOIR DU DIABLE – PRODUCTION PHOTOGRAPH.

Le MANOIR DU DIABLE

("The Devil's Manor House"; Georges Méliès, 1896-97: France)

Early in 1896 Méliès visited Hatton Garden in London, where he acquired a 35mm Theatrograph film projector from Robert W. Paul, and subsequently converted it into a camera. By May, he was making his first 20-metre films, shot at the family home in Montreuil. His first efforts – **Une Partie De Cartes** ("A Card Party") – copied from Lumière's **La Partie D'Écarte** ("The Card Party"), a film featuring *ombremane* ("shadowgraphist") Félicien Trewey – and **Séance De Prestidigitation** ("Magic Session") – were designed to further enrich the already lavish spectacles at his magic theatre, where he had already begun to include film projections using a device he named the Méliès Kinétographe. Throughout that year Méliès produced a continuous stream of films and (often accidental) cinematic innovations – **Escamotage D'Une Dame Au Théâtre Robert-Houdin** ("Conjuring A Woman At The Robert-Houdin", 1896), another early production in which a woman is transformed into a skeleton, appears to be his first use of an in-camera stop-edit. After dabbling in the documentary approach of other early film-makers, Méliès plunged straight into the production of baroque trick-phantasies. One of the earliest of these "special effects" scenarios, and his first 60-metre production, was **Le Manoir Du Diable**, a 3-minute phantasy of great historical import – almost certainly the first ever Satanic film, it can also be viewed retrospectively as the first supernatural horror film, although such genres were not then extant. The "plot", as described by Méliès himself, is simple: a large bat flies into the hall of an ancient castle and turns into Satan (played by the actor-magician Jules-Eugène Legris), who conjures a twisted gnome and a large cauldron, from which a young woman (played by actress and former nude model

Jehanne d'Alcy) arises; the gnome then presents a grimoire, which Satan reads. Hearing a noise, He retires; a lord and his servant appear, and are attacked by the gnome; the lord is soon confronted by a skeleton, which becomes the large bat which transforms back into Satan, accompanied by goblins and witches. Finally the lord seizes a holy cross and brandishes it at Satan, who flinches and vanishes in a cloud of smoke. **Le Manoir Du Diable** was released in the USA by Edison, who in 1900 advertised it under the title **The Infernal Palace**. Jules-Eugène Legris was a regular player at the Robert-Houdin, who previously portrayed Mephistopheles in an 1895 *saynète* entitled *Le Rêve De Coppelius* ("The Dream Of Coppelius"), inspired by Hoffmann. In 1897, Méliès built one of Europe's first film studios in Montreuil; refining his "diabolic" camera illusions as he went, he continued his apparent obsession with the Devil and occult themes in films such as **Le Cabinet De Méphistopheles** ("The Cabinet Of Mephistopheles", 1897), another 60-metre item in which the horned one is depicted recreating the director's range of magic transformations, **Le Château Hanté** ("The Haunted Castle", 1897), a hand-coloured 20-metre trick-scene of skeletons, ghosts and Satan, **L'Hallucination De L'Alchimiste** ("The Alchemist's Hallucination", 1897), **Faust Et Marguerite** ("Faust And Marguerite", 1897-98), a 20-metre short again starring Legris as Mephistopheles (and the film-maker's first cinematic depiction of a scene from the Faust legend), and **La Caverne Maudite** ("The Accursed Cave", 1898), with a girl accosted by ghosts and skeletons. It is perhaps notable that Pathé Frères made their first film to name-check the Devil, **Satan Contorsionniste** ("Satan The Contortionist", 1897 – possibly

BAR *L'ENFER*, PARIS, 1890s – DOCUMENTARY PHOTOGRAPH (*BELOW*.

a circus act), soon after the first screenings of **Le Manoir Du Diable**; Gaumont's first such offering, **Les Metamorphoses De Satan** – a trick-film – followed in 1898. Anticlerical, blasphemous mockery was much in vogue in the Paris of the time; this was still the era of Huysmans' decadent novel *Là-Bas*, of infernal stereoscopic photographs (*diableries*), and of Satanic cults led by the likes of Abbé Boullan. The city was renowned for a decadent fascination with the infernal and morbid; in Montmartre, drinkers could haunt such venues as *L'Enfer* ("Hell"), whose cabaret offered "diabolical attractions" and whose portal was the mouth of a huge plaster devil, or the *Cabaret du Néant* ("Cabaret of Nothingness"), decorated like a crypt with coffins, bones and other *memento mori*. As for Robert Paul back in London, he soon sold a Theatrograph to another magician, David Devant, rising young star of the Egyptian Hall; they quickly formed an alliance, with Paul producing several films of Devant's tricks in June 1896 (including **The Egg-Laying Man**). Devant also became the first British agent for the films of Georges Méliès, who officially registered the name of his Montreuil production company as Star Film in 1902.

FAUST: APPARITION DE MÉPHISTOPHÉLÈS

("Faust: Apparition Of Mephistopheles"; Lumière, 1897: France)
The first scenes depicting Faust, the folkloric figure first celebrated in literature by Christopher Marlowe and Johann Wolfgang von Goethe, were shot by Alexander Promio for Lumière, with direction by George Hatot; they also made a companion film, **Faust: Métamorphose De Faust Et Apparition De Marguerite** ("Faust: Metamorphosis Of Faust And Apparition Of Marguerite"). At around the same time Pathé Frères produced **Les Farces De Satan** ("The Tricks Of Satan"), another film of Faust selling his soul to the Devil. The legend of Faust would prove to be among the most commonly filmed in the early years of cinema. Adaptations filmed in 1898 included Georges Méliès' **Faust Et Marguerite** and **Damnation De Faust**, and George Albert Smith's **Faust And Marguerite**; these were followed by Edison's **Faust And Marguerite** (Edwin S. Porter, 1900), and Gaumont's **Faust Et Méphistophélès** ("Faust And Mephistopheles", Alice Guy, 1903).

FAUST AND MEPHISTOPHELES

(George Albert Smith, 1898: UK)
Early demonic visions by pioneer Smith. **Faust And Mephistopheles** is generally regarded as being the first British Satanic movie; its contents are reduced to one scene of Satan conjuring a vision of a girl, for whom Faust signs a pact. Another 1898 appearance by Mephistopheles was in Edwin S. Poter's horror phantasy **The**

Chevalier's Dream. Smith's **The Mesmerist**, also from 1898, uses one of the first-ever the first examples of double exposure, or superimposition to show a hypnotist drawing a girl's spirit from her body before returning it, while **Santa Claus** (also 1898) features a primitive form of split-screen. At that point, Smith and his Parisian counterpart Georges Méliès were continually outstripping each other in the invention of new cinematic tricks and camera effects. Another originary Smith work from 1898 was **Cinderella And The Fairy Godmother**, the first British "fairy-tale" film, mining a pantomime tradition which stretched back to the phantastic stage extravaganzas of James Robinson Planché, starting in 1836. Other fairy-tale films followed, including UK Mutoscope's **Daisy's Adventures In The Land Of The Chrysanthemum** (1904), Percy Stow's **Pied Piper** (1907), and Lewis Fitzhamon's **Cinderella** (1907). In 1898 Smith also made **Photographing A Ghost**, a semi-humorous "special effects" film showing an elusive phantom which, when released from its box, refuses to stay still for the camera. The following year Smith assumed charge of a range of films produced by Warwick Trading Company for their new Biokam camera-projector, with 17.5 mm Biokam films being produced for the domestic market in one of the earliest examples of amateur cine/home projection technologies. One surviving example of the Biokam catalogue is **Hey, Diddle Diddle, The Cat And The Fiddle** (c.1901), a Méliès-style visual recreation of an old nursery-rhyme, with an anthropomorphic moon and characters in animal costumes.

Le DIABLE AU COUVENT
("The Devil In A Convent"; Georges Méliès, 1899: France)
An important precedent in the history of cinema, as Méliès directs the first film to deal with the subject of a cursed convent and nuns tempted or possessed by the Devil, a later exploitation film staple. Satan (played by Méliès himself) manifests in a convent and proceeds to corrupt the sisters in the guise of a charming priest, before

LE DIABLE AU COUVENT – PRODUCTION PHOTOGRAPH.

being exorcised and driven out. The 60-metre film is split into three scenarios: *Les Nonnes, Le Sermon* ("Nuns: The Sermon"); *Les Démons, Le Sabbat* ("Demons: The Sabbat"); and *Le Clergé, L'Exorcisme* ("Priests: The Exorcism"). A gigantic toad and a huge cat's head also appear; the climactic scenes also mark **Le Diable Au Couvent** as the first exorcist movie. Another diabolic Méliès film *saynète* from 1899 was **Le Miroir De Cagliostro** ("Cagliostro's Mirror"), with a girl morphing into a skeleton and then a huge head of Satan.

PIERROT BUVEUR
("Pierrot The Drinker"; Parnaland, 1900: France)
At under one minute in duration, this Méliès-style invocation of Mephistopheles depicts the alcoholic hallucination of a portly *pierrot*, who is visited by the infernal Master after downing a bottle of wine. As Mephistopheles torments the terrified clown, His head turns into that of a wolf in a brilliant flash of metamorphic trans-species horror. As in Méliès' **Manoir Du Diable**, He is finally repelled by a crucifix-wielding nun.

Les SEPT CHÂTEAUX DU DIABLE
("Seven Castles Of The Devil"; Ferdinand Zecca, 1901: France)
This originary *féerie satanique* ranks among the most elaborate of Pathé's trick-phantasy films. Its title presumably derives from a 3-act theatre production of the same name by Adolphe Dennery et Charles Clairville, which first played at the Théâtre de la Gaîté in Paris in 1844, and the story also references the legend of Faust (whose signature can be seen in the Devil's book of compacts). With an original duration of around twenty minutes, **Les Sept Châteaux Du Diable** opens in Satan's infernal laboratory where, assisted by the demon Astaroth, He holds a midnight Sabbat of witches, before the witches are plunged into a vast cauldron already boiling with snakes. Seven beautiful women emerge, each representing one of the seven mortal sins: Wrath, Sloth, Lust, Envy, Greed, Gluttony and Pride. Satan shows them their appointed victim, a poverty-stricken and suicidal woodcutter named Fridolin, and they depart. Easily tempted by the beautiful demons, he signs away his soul; his shack is transformed into a palace, and Fridolin is taken away to be crowned King in a ceremony conducted by Satan in disguise. Meanwhile his discarded fiancée, Brigitte, is helped by Isoline, a good fairy, who gives her a magic talisman. Fridolin is now plunged into a career of evil and vice, immersed in all the horrors of the seven sins and continually goaded by Satan. The castle of Gluttony is particularly effective, showing a huge face devouring a whole roast pig followed by several small children. Statues representing Lust and Sloth turn into beautiful harem-girls, and many other metamorphoses unfurl before the hour arrives when Satan will claim the deranged wood-cutter's soul. Fridolin joins a sorry parade of other lost souls on the River Styx, and the Devil's castle looms over this demon-infested swamp that laps at the shores of Hell. At the last minute Brigitte and the fairy Isoline intevene, repelling Satan in a scene represented by St. George slaying the dragon. One of Pathé's longest *féerie* productions, a major entry in the history of Satanic cinema, and clearly an attempt to surpass the increasingly ambitious projects of Georges Méliès – as an obvious elaboration of Méliès' **Sept Péchés Capitaux** from the previous year – Zecca's film featured set décor by Albert Colas and comprised an epic forty *tableaux*.[1] Two much more modest trick-films from Zecca in the same year were the 20-metre **Le Repas Infernal** ("The Infernal Feast") and the 30-metre **Une Tempête Dans Une Chambre À Coucher** ("Storm In A Bed-Room").

1. The forty *tableaux* were: *Le Laboratoire infernal* ("The infernal laboratory"); *Astaroth, génie du feu, présente à Satan la torche diabolique* ("Astaroth, the fire demon, hands Satan the diabolic torch"); *Évocation et danse du feu* ("Invocation and fire-dance"); *La chaudière infernale* ("The infernal cauldron"); *Le Sabbat. Entrée et danse des sorcières* ("The Sabbat: arrival and dance of the witches"); *Satan crée les Sept Péchés capitaux* ("Satan creates the Seven Deadly Sins"); *Apparition De Fridolin* ("Apparition of Fridolin"); *Satan ordonne aux Sept Péchés capitaux d'aller le tenter* ("Satan orders The Seven Deadly Sins to go and tempt him"); *La chaumière de Fridolin* ("Fridolin's cottage"); *Satan lui apparaît et lui offre, en échange de son âme, les plaisirs et la fortune* ("Satan appears and offers him wealth and pleasure in exchange for his soul", three *tableaux*); *Fridolin signe le pacte* ("Fridolin signs the pact"); *Au Château de*

l'Envie ("In the Castle of Envy"); *Changé en un riche seigneur, Fridolin est choisi comme roi* ("Now a rich lord, Fridolin is chosen as king"); *Au Château de l'Orgueil* ("In the Castle of Pride"); *Entrée de Fridolin et de sa cour* ("Arrival of Fridolin and his court"); *Le Couronnement* ("The Coronation"); *Grand défilé des Décorations* ("Grand procession of Honours"); *Ballet de l'Orgueil* ("Ballet of Pride"); *Fridolin désavoue sa fiancée Brigitte* (Fridolin disavows his betrothed, Brigitte); *Apparition de la fée Isoline, elle remet à Brigitte le talisman qui doit sauver Fridolin* ("Apparition of the fairy Isoline, who gives Brigitte a talisman which can save Fridolin", two *tableaux*); *Au Château de l'Avarice* ("In the Castle of Greed"); *Fridolin est dépouillé de ses trésors par des brigands* ("Fridolin is stripped of his treasures by robbers"); *Au Château de la Colère* ("In the Castle of Wrath"); *Les Métamorphoses de Satan* ("The Metamorphoses of Satan"); *Explosion et destruction du Château de la Colère* ("Detonation and destruction of the Castle of Wrath"); *La Dévastation* ("Devastation"); *Au Pays de Cocagne, le Château de la Gourmandise* (In the land of Cocagne, the Castle of Greed"); *Le Repas de Gargantua* ("Gargantua's feast"); *L'Armée des Marmitons. Défilé* ("The army of kitchen-boys: procession"); *Poursuite des Apothicaires* (Chasing the apothecaries"); *Au Château de la Paresse* ("In the Castle of Sloth"); *Ballet de la Luxure* ("Ballet of Lust"); *Sur le Styx, la route des Enfers* ("On the Styx, the pathway to Hell"); *Convoi des Damnés* ("Convoy of the damned"); *Fridolin est emmené aux Enfers* ("Fridolin is ferried to Hell"); *Le Royaume de Satan* ("Satan's realm""); and *Triomphe de Brigitte. Apothéose* ("Brigitte's triumph: grand climax"). An edited, hand-coloured 11-minute version appears to have been prepared for overseas release in 1903 or 1904.

La MARMITE DIABOLIQUE
("The Diabolic Cooking-Pot"; Gaston Velle, 1902: France)
Velle, a stage magician and pioneering director with an eye for the supernatural, was the driving force behind Lumière's **Nouvelles Vues Fantasmagoriques** ("New Phantasmagoric Scenes") series, shot between 1902 and 1903. In **La Marmite Diabolique**, a farce which combines Satanic elements with corporeal destruction, a busy cook accidentally hurls his pantry-boy into a pot of boiling stew; when he fishes him out, the boy has no head. The cook replaces his head with a cabbage, but then the Devil emerges from the cooking-pot and scares the cook away. After reviving the boy, the Devil catches the cook and plunges him into the boiling pot. Velle's other offerings in this Lumière series included **Arlequin Et Méphistophélès** ("Harlequin And Mephistopheles"), **Le Château Hanté** ("The Haunted Castle"), and **Le Repas Fantastique** ("The Phantastic Feast") – the last-mentioned featuring a pantry-boy with the head of a calf, a lobster which turns into a rabbit, and other gastro-demonic marvels. Velle moved to Pathé Frères in 1904, and was most likely the director of their remake of **La Marmite Diabolique** that year, retaining the same title and plot elements, but moving to another level of physical destruction and devilry. These antics were also mirrored in a 1904 Méliès production, **Sorcellerie Culinaire** ("Culinary Sorcery"); Méliès' other films of kitchen mayhem notably included **La Cuisine D'Ogre** ("The Ogre's Kitchen", 1907), a typical example of corporeal dissolution which introduces the theme of cannibalism as an ogre kills, butchers and mashes a young man into paste to devour his body parts. As with many such early films, the finale sees a mystic apparition, whose gnomes exact vengeance on the flesh-eater in his grotesque cavern of human bones by roasting him over his own fire.

Le CAKE-WALK INFERNAL
("Infernal Cake-Walk"; Georges Méliès, 1903: France)
A 100-metre *satanique* in which demons, dancers and black-face cake-carriers perform the popular, paroxysmal "Cake-Walk" cavort in a blazing inferno, and a deformed, hunch-backed devil jumps out of a gigantic *gâteau*. Soon, even the fires of Hell are dancing along as if possessed. Satan finally appears and banishes the revellers from His kingdom. That same year Méliès completed another Hell-dance film, **Les Filles Du Diable** ("The Devil's Daughters") – Satan conjures up a blazing fire, and from the flames emerge three girls who proceed to dance, whilst two demons shake burning torches; the figures then all disappear. Pathé joined in the fun with **Le Cake-Walk Chez Les Nains** ("Cake-Walk In Dwarf-Land", also made in 1903), but unfortunately no real dwarfs are used in this film; instead, trick photography shows us tiny figures dancing in the palm of a man's hand. The Cake-Walk, renowned for its wild abandon and limb-shaking, was often likened to epilepsy or the gyrating of savages by its detractors; it derived from the antics of the *gommeuses épileptiques* of late 19th century Paris cabaret, garishly-apparelled singers whose acts were marked by physical contortions inspired by the medical photographs of Jean-Martin Charcot. Méliès continued with **Le Chaudron Infernal** ("The Devil's Cauldron"), a 40-metre

hand-coloured short also made in 1903, in which two demons hurl three women into a blazing brazier; the roasted women emerge as nebulous spectres which turn into fireballs.

FAUST AUX ENFERS
("Faust In Hell"; Georges Méliès, 1903: France)

Méliès' third Faust film was a 145-metre feast of infernal visions based on *La Damnation De Faust* by Hector Berlioz, running for an approximate 6- or 7-minute duration. The film was constructed as a series of fifteen diabolic *tableaux*, whose titles were listed in the American Méliès catalogue as: "The Route To The Depths Of Perdition", "The Fantastical Ride", "The Gloomy Pass", "The Stream", "The Entrance To The Lower Regions", "The Marvelous Grottoes", "The Crystal Stalactites", "The Devil's Hole", "The Ice Cavern", "The Goddesses Of Antiquity", "The Subterranean Cascade", "The Nymphs Of The Underworld – The Seven Headed Hydra – The Demons – The Struggle Of Water With Fire", "The Descent To Satan's Domain", "The Furnace", and "The Triumph Of Mephistopheles". The official American release title was actually **The Damnation Of Faust**. Some of the film's visual highlights include a weird seven-headed monster, prancing masked demons, a vertiginous fall into the Inferno, and a climactic scene (or apotheosis) in which Mephistopheles (played by Méliès himself) stands gloating and triumphant, with cloaked arms outspread over his subjects. **The Condemnation Of Faust** (Lubin, 1904) was reportedly a straight pirate of **Faust Aux Enfers**.

LA DAMNATION DU DOCTEUR FAUST – PRODUCTION
PHOTOGRAPH.

La DAMNATION DU DOCTEUR FAUST
("The Damnation Of Doctor Faust"; Georges Méliès, 1904: France)
Méliès' obsession with the legend of Faust and Mephistopheles reached its apotheosis
with this crowning 260-metre spectacle in twenty *tableaux*, based on Gounod's opera
Faust and the famous novel by Goethe. The film's scenes included Faust's laboratory,
the apparition and bargain of the Devil (played by Méliès), and a vivid recreation of
the black rites of Walpurgisnacht (the first depiction in cinema of the Witches Sabbat).
The 14-minute work was released in America as **Faust And Marguerite**. Another
Satanic film made by Méliès in 1904 was **Les Invités De M. Latourte** ("Mr. Latourte's
Guests"), in which the Devil gate-crashes a man's birthday dinner. Subsequent film
derivations of the Faust legend include Alice Guy's **Faust** (1906);[1] Gaston Velle's **Patto
Infernale** ("Infernal Pact", 1907);[2] Selig's **Faust** (1908); Pathé's **Mademoiselle Faust**
("Miss Faust", 1909 – with trick photography by Segundo de Chomón); **Faust**
(Edwin S. Porter, 1909); Pathé's **Faust** (Henri Andréani, 1910); **Faust** (Enrico
Guazzoni, 1910); Jean Durand's **Faust Et Marguerite** (Gaumont, 1911); Pathé's **Faust
Sauvé Des Enfers** ("Faust Saved From Hell", 1911);[3] and **Faust** (Edward Sloman,
1915). The most unusual Faust films of this period may be Emile Cohl's 6-minute
puppet animation **Le Tout Petit Faust** ("The Tiny Little Faust", 1910), a stop-motion
experiment, and Essanay's **Bill Bumper's Bargain** (1911), a parody starring Francis
X. Bushman as Mephisto.

1. This Gaumont production was comprised of over twenty *photoscènes*, short films with a soundtrack
registered on wax cylinder; Guy reportedly made over 400 such films between 1903 and 1906.
Photoscènes were created using chronophonic technology developed by Gaumont since 1900. **Faust – À**

Moi Les Plaisirs! ("Faust – The Pleasures Are Mine!", 1908) was a *scène ciné-phonographique* from Pathé. Other musical versions from this period include British Gaumont's **Faust** (1907), directed by Arthur Gilbert and screened using chronophonic synching; **Kerkerszene Aus Faust** ("Prison Scene From Faust", 1909), a *tonbild* from Deutsche Mutoskop; **Faust: Soldatenchor. Nr. 79** ("Faust: Soldiers' Choir No. 79", 1909), a *tonbild* from Deutsche Bioscop; **Faust** (1910), a *tonbild* from Messter; and Cecil M. Hepworth's **Faust** (1911), with the synchronised Vivaphone recording system.

2. **Patto Infernale**, produced for Cines, was a remake of Velle's earlier Pathé film, **Le Secret De L'Horloger** ("The Clock-Maker's Secret").

3. Pathé's later films of this nature included **La Sonnette Du Diable** ("The Devil's Chimes", 1916), based on a phantasmagoric play of Satanic soul-selling first staged in 1849.

L'AMOUREUX ENSORCELÉ – PRODUCTION PHOTOGRAPH.

L'AMOUREUX ENSORCELÉ
("The Bewitched Lover"; Ferdinand Zecca, 1905: France)
Another of Pathé's many films involving the Devil and witchcraft, based on the familiar tale of Satan infiltrating a man's household in the guise of a beggar.[1] Once inside his victim's home He wreaks havoc, finally driving the man to such rage and madness that his fiancée, coveted by Satan, has him arrested by two policemen.

1. Zecca, who moved to Pathé from Gaumont, had no compunction about remaking films made by his former company; **L'Amoureux Ensorcelé** is basically a copy of Gaumont's **Fiancé Ensorcelé** (1903).

La MALIA DELL'ORO
("The Enchantment Of Gold"; Filoteo Alberini, 1905: Italy)
Seemingly inspired by the infernal phantasies of Georges Méliès and other French film-makers, **La Malia Dell'Oro** is amongst the very first works of Italian cinema, and the country's first film fantasy. Comprising six *quadri* (scenes), the film tells how a penurious painter's obsession with gold leads him on a profane quest into Hell, confronting Satan, before he is rescued by the Goddess of Fortune. A musical score written by Romolo Bacchini specifically to accompany the film – to be played by a live orchestra during screenings – is regarded as the cinema's first such composition. The following year, director Alberini – a film pioneer, inventor and exhibitor since 1894 – founded the film company Cines, a prolific producer and distributor until 1921. After some initial trick-films, which included the Satanic short **Pierrot All'Inferno** ("Pierrot In Hell", 1906), Cines began to specialise in historical dramas. Some other notable fantasy and trick-films from the primal years of Italian cinema included Gaston Velle's **Le Avventure Di Pulcinella** ("The Adventures Of Pulcinella", 1907), **Leggenda Di San Nicola** ("The Legend Of Saint Nicholas", 1907, from Rossi & C.), **La Bacchetta Del Diavolo** ("The Devil's Ring", 1909, from Cines), and Azeglio Pineschi's **Il Pittore E Il Diavolo** ("The Painter And The Devil", 1909), in which an artist finally finds inspiration when Satan shows him the colours of Hell – but demands a high price in return.

LA POULE AUX OEUFS D'OR – PRODUCTION PHOTOGRAPH.

La POULE AUX OEUFS D'OR
("The Hen With Golden Eggs"; Gaston Velle, 1905: France)
Velle collaborated with special effects genius Segundo de Chomón to create this 4-part, 12-*tableau*, hand-coloured *conte féerie* for Pathé, based on an old fable by Jean

de La Fontaine. In Part One, *La Loterie Du Sorcier* ("The Sorcerer's Lottery"), a conjuror gives a white hen to a farmer, the lucky winner of his wheel-of-fortune game. In Part Two, *Le Poulailler Fantastique* ("The Amazing Chicken-Coop"), the magic hen starts to produce golden eggs filled with coins, and all the chickens in the coop turn into feather-costumed dancing-girls. In Part Three, *Richesse Éphémère* ("Ephemeral Wealth"), the owners of the magic hen have acquired great riches and live in a palace, but a curse falls upon them; the face of Satan appears on an egg, presaging all manner of strange visitations, apparitions and calamities. In the fourth and final part, or apotheosis, *Le Châtiment De L'Avare* ("Punishment Of The Miser"), Satan appears and urges the farmer to kill his magic hen; he does so, and searches inside its entrails for more gold. A spirit appears, chastising him. The film ends with the barn transformed into a gilded wonderland, but the farmer is driven away by the feathered girls as a rain of gold closes the proceedings. With its Satanic overtones, weird visions, lavish set designs and startling effects, **La Poule Aux Oeufs D'Or** stands near the pinnacle of Pathé's faery-film phantasies. Segundo de Chomón's **L'Araignée D'Or** ("The Golden Spider", 1908) was a weird and somewhat horrific variant on the same moralistic fable; it involves a sect of robed and hooded monks who have discovered a large spider which spins golden coins. A wood-cutter steals the spider, but when his greed overpowers his humanity, his newly-minted wealth rots into a mass of writhing vermin.

Le FILS DU DIABLE À PARIS
("The Devil's Son In Paris"; Charles-Lucien Lépine; 1906: France)
One of the earliest films to star André Deed, an extremely popular French screen comedian, is a crude comedy showing the son of Satan seducing a young girl in the big city, leading to her suicide. Special trick effects were by Segundo de Chomón. A similar film was Louis Feuillade's Gaumont production **Satan Fait La Noce** ("Satan's Wedding", 1907). André Deed first appeared as a *pierrot* in the Georges Méliès special-effects "dismantled body" short **Dislocations Mystérieuses** ("Strange Dislocations", 1901), before joining Pathé in 1905. Some of his most successful films for the company involved the grotesque character of Boireau, a character seeded in the classic absurdist chase-film **La Course À La Perruque** ("The Wig Chase", 1906)[1] and first named in Georges Hatot's **Boireau Déménage** ("Boireau Moves House", 1906); the Boireau comedies were marked by increasingly spectacular acrobatic feats. In 1909 Deed relocated to Italy, becoming "Cretinetti" (renamed "Gribouille" for French release) in a series of films for Itala, but returned to Pathé in 1912 to film another lengthy series of deranged Boireau adventures.[2] He went back to Italy in 1915, directing a series of new projects with generally diminishing success.

1. The comic chase-film in France first took shape with Georges Hatot's **Dix Femmes Pour Un Mari** ("Ten Women For One Husband", 1905), itself a direct remodel/copy of Wallace McCutcheon's highly influential **Personal** (USA, 1904).

2. Notably **Une Extraordinaire Aventure De Boireau** (1914), in which Boireau needs a wood-cutter's saw to surgically detach himself from a violent criminal after their flesh is welded together by a high-velocity impact.

Les QUAT'CENTS FARCES DU DIABLE
("The Devil's Four Hundred Tricks"; Georges Méliès, 1906: France)
Based on the 1905 stage-play *Les Quatre Cents Coups Du Diable* ("The Devil's 400 Shocks") by Victor de Cottens and Victor Darlay, Méliès' most complex and refined excursion into Satanic cinema is an epic *féerie satanique*, with thirty-five *tableaux* presenting a whole series of visual transformations and phantasmic constructs: an alchemical laboratory of huge athanors and retorts, the Devil materialising in a church, two demons connecting a series of trunks into a diabolic train, the Devil's coach being drawn through the stars by a skeletal horse and trailing comets and suns in its wake, and a climactic, hand-tinted vision of Hell with the Devil roasting in his own infernal glory.[1] At 445 metres, **Les Quat'Cents Farces Du Diable** was by far Méliès' longest and most ambitious Satanic film production. Méliès' next portrayal of the Devil came with **Satan En Prison** ("Satan In Prison", 1907).

LES QUAT'CENTS FARCES DU DIABLE – MÉLIÈS AS MEPHISTO (*OPPOSITE PAGE*).

LES QUAT'CENTS FARCES DU DIABLE – PRODUCTION PHOTOGRAPH.

1. According to Méliès, the contents of film's thirty-five *tableaux* were: *Le cabinet del'ingénieur William Crackford* ("The office of the engineer William Crackford"); *L'enyoyé de Satan. Le juif Kaulsbach* ("Satan's envoy. The Jew Kualsbach"); *Le laboratoire du diable* ("The Devil's laboratory"); *Le mobilier satanique* ("The Satanic furniture"); *L'alchimiste Alcofrisbas* ("Alcofrisbas the alchemist"); *Les supports de Satan (les sept péchés capitaux)* ("Satan's tools – the Seven Deadly Sins"); *Les pilules du diable. La fée et le monstre* ("The Devil's pills. The fairy and the monster"); *La salle á manger de W. Crackford* ("W. Crackford's dining-room"); *Les malles infernales et les domestiques de Pluton* ("The infernal trunks and Pluto's servants"); *Un déménagement fantastique* ("A fantastic removal"); *Le train diabolique* ("The diabolic train"); *Dans les ruines de Londres* ("In the ruins of London"); *La population s'ameute* ("The people rise up"); *Le torrent et le ravin. Dans les Alpes* ("The torrent and the ravine. In the Alps."); *La catastrophe* ("The catastrophe"); *Forward!!!* ("Forward!!!"); *La place du village de Montépépéto (Italie)* ("The Montépépéto village square, Italy"); *Le débarquement* ("Landing"); *La salle d'auberge ensorcelée (les démons)* ("The bewitched inn-chamber – demons"); *La cuisine, les farces du diable* ("The kitchen, the Devil's tricks"); *La diligence et le postillon* ("The stagecoach and the coachman"); *Le cheval apocalyptique et la voiture astrale* ("The apocalyptic horse and the astral car"); *Satan en automobile* ("Satan at the wheel"); *La montée du Vésuve* ("Mount Vesusvius"); *L'eruption volcanique* ("The volcanic eruption"); *Dans les nuages, la chevauchée fantastique* ("In the clouds, the wild ride"); *Les astres vivants* ("The living stars"); *Un orage de feu* ("A storm of fire"); *Effroyable chute dans le vide* ("Dreadful plunge into the abyss"); *La parachute, retour à terre* ("The parachute, return to the ground"); *À travers les toits et planchers* ("Through the roofs and floors"); *L'échéance fatale* ("The fatal date"); *La descente aux enfers. Le Styx* ("Descent into Hell. The Styx"); *Les divinités infernales. Ballet* ("The infernal deities. Ballet"); and *Le tournebroche du diable* ("The Devil's spit-roaster").

LE SPECTRE ROUGE – PRODUCTION PHOTOGRAPH (*ABOVE*).

Le SPECTRE ROUGE

("The Red Spectre"; Segundo de Chomón, 1907: France)

In a subterranean lair, a demonic sorcerer plays with the souls of captive women, capturing them in glass bottles. A beautifully hand-coloured film, with each frame individually painted, and enhanced by wild trick effects and diabolic settings – a brilliant exemplar of early film alchemy and terror. Chomón was also director of photography for Gaston Velle's **L'Antre Infernal** ("The Devil's Lair", 1905), in which Satan conjures up two wanton women in Hell. Velle and Chomón would invoke Satan again in the Pathé production **Le Secret De L'Horloger** ("The Clock-Maker's Secret", 1907), in which the horned one is repulsed by a crucifix-wielding virgin when coming to claim the soul of her father, an elderly clock-maker. And Chomón came back that same year with **Satan S'Amuse** ("Satan At Play"), drawing heavily on **Le Spectre Rouge**. Pathé would continue producing this type of infernal film, with works such as **Les Trois Péchés Du Diable** ("The Devil's Three Sins", 1908), Chomón's **La Forge Infernale** ("The Infernal Forge", 1908) and **La Forge Du Diable** ("The Devil's Forge", 1909), **Le Philtre Maudit** ("The Accursed Potion", 1909), **La Défaite De Satan** ("Satan Defeated", 1910), and the 15-*tableau* **Rival De Satan** ("Satan's Rival", directed by Gérard Bourgeois and starring Georges Wague as Satan, 1911). Bourgeois had previously made **La Vente Du Diable** ('The Devil's Auction", 1908) for Lux; Éclipse also joined in the infernal revelry with **Satan S'Ennuie** ("Satan Is Bored", 1911) – released in the USA as **Satan On A Rampage** – in which the Horned One, tiring of Hell, invades Paris and snatches up a beautiful young bride, dragging her down into the Pit. Chomón's **La Grotte Des Esprits** ("Cave Of Souls",

1909) was a slight variation on the theme, presenting infernal scenes of cavorting
skeletons in an evocation of the artist Hans Holbein's famous woodcut series *Les
Simulachres Et Historiées Faces De La Mort* ("Images And Illustrated Faces Of
Death", published in 1538 and known in English as *The Dance Of Death*). 1906
saw the first of several wild "witch" films by Chomón, the 6-part **La Dernière
Sorcière** ("The Last Witch"), which was followed by **L'Antre De La Sorcière** ("The
Witch's Cavern", also 1906), **Le Baiser De La Sorcière** ("The Witch's Kiss", 1907),
Le Secret De La Sorcière ("The Witch's Secret", also 1907), and **L'Ane De La Sorcière**
("The Witch's Donkey", 1909); all these films are filled with the director's customary
visual tricks, grotesqueries and Satanic flourishes.

THE DEVIL
(D.W. Griffith, 1908: USA)
A grim parable from American Mutoscope, featuring George Gebhardt as Satan,
tempting a married artist into fornication with one of his models. When his wife tries
to get even by flirting – again urged by the Devil – the husband flies into a rage and,
obeying Satan's final orders to kill, shoots her dead before taking his own life. Based
on the sensational play *Az Ördög* ("The Devil") by Hungarian author Ferenc Molnár,
one of numerous film adaptations of which another was by Edwin S. Porter who
presented his own **The Devil**, a similar tale of diabolic temptation and adultery, the
same year. Satan featured again in pioneering director J. Stuart Blackton's **The
Gambler And The Devil**, in which a gambling addict plays dice with the Devil for

THE DEVIL – PAPER PRINT PRODUCTION PHOTOGRAPH.

his wife's soul. Later in 1908 Vitagraph produced a skit, **He Went To See The Devil Play**, in which a man goes to watch a stage play of *The Devil*,[1] gets drunk, and starts hallucinating that everyone he meets turns into Satan.

1. Starring stage actor George Arliss as Satan; Arliss would reprise the role in **The Devil** (1920), his first film appearance.

La LÉGENDE DU FANTÔME
("The Legend Of The Ghost"; Segundo de Chomón, 1908: France)
Chomón's deluge of infernal trick-cinema is a hand-dyed optical explosion of demonic and supernatural pantomime imagery, filled with strange creatures and devils in occult grottoes. Although its "plot" is visually incomprehensible, production company Pathé's synopsis indicates a trip into Hell and a pyrotechnic battle with Satan, in order to retrieve the "flame of life", an elixir which will revert a mournful ghost to flesh-and-blood. The weird trip then moves into an undersea realm, where the "black pearl" is guarded by a bevy of saturated sirens and bizarre hybrid creatures, and ends with mass murder by way of infernal retribution. Regardless of interpretation, this 13-minute *féerie satanique* stands as a relentless riot of hellfire hallucinations, a carnivalesque cavort through the history of dark human dreams. Another Satanic film created by Chomón in 1908 was **Les Flammes Mystérieuses** ('The Mysterious Flames"), in which the Devil is portrayed as a conjuror performing fiery tricks.

DAMNATION

MP des ETAB^{ts} PATHÉ FRERES 14, Rue FAVART · PARIS ·   ATELIER · FARIA · 6 Rue Steinkerque · PARIS ·

CUORE DI MAMMA
("Mother's Heart"; Luigi Maggi, 1909: Italy)

One of Ambrosio's key Satanic narratives from their formative years, with cinematography from Giovanni Vitrotti and a promotional poster, beautifully illustrated by Roberto Omegna, showing the Devil with a human heart between His fingertips. As this image indicates, Maggi's extraordinary phantasy involves a woman who is visited by Satan in human guise; when she rejects His sexual advances, He reveals his true form and steals her heart from her body – leaving her emotionless and blank. Her daughter, desperate to restore love to her mother's soul, is advised to seek out the Devil's castle, armed only with a magic veil. After overcoming a succession of obstacles, imprisonment, demons and witches, she finally reaches Satan's throne room and is able to retrieve her mother's heart while He sleeps. Another 1909 production which dealt with Satan manipulating human emotions was the Pathé Frères production **Damnation**. In this short film fable the Devil is jealous of a newly wed couple and tricks them into betrayal. The story ends in murder and, as its title implies, an eternal descent into Hell.

CUORE DI MAMMA – FILM POSTER (*ABOVE*).
DAMNATION – FILM POSTER BY ATELIER FARIA (*OPPOSITE PAGE*).

HELVEDES DATTER – PRODUCTION PHOTOGRAPH.

HELVEDES DATTER
("Daughter Of Hell"; Nordisk, 1909: Denmark)

This short film, whose director (possibly Viggo Larsen) is unconfirmed, features an infernal vision in the style of Méliès; surviving photographs and posters depict vivid scenes in Hell, where an artist dreams he is being persecuted by she-devils with pitchforks. This scene of torment is presided over by the figure of Satan himself, against a painted backdrop of grotesque skulls, corpses and serpents. Released in Germany as **Das Höllenkind** ("The Hell-Child").

COME FU CHE L'INGORDIGIA ROVINÒ IL NATALE A CRETINETTI

("How Greed Ruined Cretinetti's Christmas"; Itala Film, 1910: Italy)

In 1908, French film comic André Deed – already known as the Pathé character Boireau – relocated to Italy, where he created a new absurdist slapstick screen persona, Cretinetti, for Itala Film. January 1909 saw the release of **Cretinetti Re Dei Poliziotti** ("Cretinetti, King Of Cops"), the first in a lengthy series of short films based on extreme situations and behaviour, characterised by destruction of both objects and the human body. The films often featured special effects such as stop-motion animation, and the "plots" verged on chaos. Cretinetti was anarchy and nonsense personnified, and was gleefully destroyed himself in several films, such as **Cretinetti E Le Donne** ("Cretinetti And The Women", 1909), where he was torn limb from limb by a gaggle of lust-crazed women. Released two days before Christmas 1910, **Come Fu Che L'Ingordigia Rovinò Il Natale A Cretinetti** stands out from this mass of mayhem by its bizarre dream narrative and scenes in Heaven and Hell, a nightmarish trip caused by Cretinetti's over-eating – for which he is duly punished and tortured by Satan and his pitchfork-wielding minions.

CORSA NEGLI ABISSI
("Race To The Abyss"; Milano Films, 1910: Italy)

An experimental film, made specifically to be screened during a performance of Hector Berlioz's Satanic opera *La Damnation De Faust* ("The Damnation Of Faust") at Milan's Teatro La Scala in February 1910. The race to the abyss comes at the opera's climax, when Faust is led on horseback by Mephistopheles into the pit of Pandemonium, the place of all demons – otherwise known as Hell. The mixing of film and theatre was also essayed in other countries during this period, notably in Japan where it was known as *rensa-geki* ("chain-drama"). The Cines production **Faust**, also released in 1910, was a more direct film rendition of the original story by Goethe, directed by Enrico Guazzoni and praised for its lavish production values.

The DEVIL, THE SERVANT AND THE MAN
(Frank Beal, 1910: USA)

In this typically sensational Selog Polyscope production, a gad-about husband is visited by the Devil in his drunken dreams; the Devil leads him to various locations and shows him that wife is repeatedly unfaithful. He also gives the man a loaded revolver. Finally, seeing his wife at a masked ball in the arms of another man, the husband snaps and shoots her dead. When he awakes, confused, he believes he has murdered his wife and is only stopped from blowing out his own brains by his faithful servant, who assures him it was all a nightmare. For some reason Beal directed two remakes/variations of this film, both for Selig, in 1912 and again in 1916. Selig conjured Satan again in **The Devil And Tom Walker** (1913), a supernatural period

THE DEVIL AND TOM WALKER - PRODUCTION PHOTOGRAPH.

drama in which the infernal majesty was played by William Stowell; in this adaptation of a Washington Irving short story, a man sells his soul in exchange for the buried treasure of the pirate Captain Kidd. When he finally tires of carrying out the Devil's pranks, only a bible can protect him; but the holy book is stolen, and Tom is carried off to Hell. **The Devil** (1910) was a Powers Picture Plays farce about a man who attends a masquerade dressed as Satan, gets drunk, and subsequently terrorizes the neighbourhood. The actual Devil was depicted in Lubin's farce **Fountain Of Youth** (1911), and also in Thanhouser's **The Tempter And Dan Cupid** (also 1911), a phantasy in which Satan corrupts a young man away from his fiancée with gambling and loose women, but is finally defeated by the love angel. And in Solax's **Strangers From Nowhere** (1913), two mysterious figures – Satan and Conscience – do battle over a sinful woman's soul.

Il DIAVOLO ZOPPO
("The Crippled Devil"; Luigi Maggi, 1910: Italy)
Another Satanic film by Maggi and Società Ambrosio, this time adapting the 1707 French novel *Le Diable Boiteux* by Alain-René Lesage. The film's story concerns a young man, Leandro (played by Ernesto Vaser), who frees the bottled demon Asmodeus (Ercole Vaser) from captivity in an alchemist's lair; in return the demon enables Leandro to fly with him over the town's rooftops where, with a special looking-glass, he can see into every house. Maggi concentrates on two episodes, ending with Leandro marrying a wealthy princess who the demon (assuming Leandro's form) rescues from a fire. With cinematography by Giovanni Vitrotti, **Il Diavolo Zoppo** is one of Italian cinema's key early films of trickery and diabolism, remarkable for its various special effects; it was released in the USA as **The Devil On Two Sticks**, one of many European items imported by New York Motion Picture in 1909-1910.

IL DEMONE
("The Demon"; Giovanni Vitrotti & F. Korfus, 1911: Italy/Russia)
This rare collaboration between Ambrosio Film of Turin and Moscow's Timan & Reyngardt was just one of several films of the supernatural to be screened in Italy in 1911. The 12-minute film is based upon the famous Luciferian poem of the same name by Mikhail Lermontov, written in 1829-39, in which a demonic fallen angel wanders the earth in a doomed quest for love. At the poem's climax, which inspired a famous painting by Russian artist Mikhail Vrubel, the princess Tamara is killed by the demon's deadly kiss. Vrubel's numerous imagistic evocations of the poem were undoubtedly a key visual guide for the makers of **Il Demone**.

IL DEMONE – PRODUCTION PHOTOGRAPH.

LES HALLUCINATIONS DU BARON DE MÜNCHAUSEN –
PRODUCTION PHOTOGRAPH.

Les HALLUCINATIONS DU BARON DE MÜNCHAUSEN

("The Hallucinations Of Baron Münchausen"; Georges Méliès, 1911: France)
Running for 235 metres, **Les Hallucinations Du Baron De Münchausen** was the first
of six film projects directed by Méliès for Pathé Frères, and the first film based on
the 1786 story-book *Baron Munchausen's Narrative Of His Marvellous Travels And
Campaigns In Russia* by Rudolf Erich Raspe, a satirical suite of outlandish adventures
(including travelling to the moon). Typically, Méliès mainly used the idea of the book
as springboard for his own imagination, depicting a series of bizarre dreams induced
by excessive alcohol consumption. Other films based on Raspe's book followed,
including Émile Cohl's animation **Monsieur De Crac** (1912), Paolo Azzurri's **Le
Avventure Del Barone Di Münchausen** ("The Adventures Of Baron Münchausen",
1914) and F. Martin Thornton's **The New Adventures Of Baron Munchausen** (1915).
Scenes in **Les Hallucinations Du Baron De Münchausen** include the familar figure of
Mephistopheles, and in his final Pathé-produced films Méliès would reference his
former Satanic roles by once again depicting a demon-afflicted alchemist in **Le Vitrail
Diabolique** ("The Devilish Stained-Glass Window", 1911), and by portraying the
demon Belphegor in **Le Chevalier Des Neiges** ("The Snow Knight", 1912 – promoted
as a "fantastic children's fairy-tale").[1]

1. Méliès' influence can be seen in the USA as late as 1914, when Edison produced **Fantasma**, an
adaptation of an 1884 stage phantasmagoria; the film starred W.T. Carleton, renowned for his operatic
portrayals of Mephistopheles, as a similar figure of evil named Zamliel, who rises from Hell accompanied
by a retinue of cavorting imps and demons.

L'INFERNO - PRINTED PRODUCTION PHOTOGRAPHS. THESE LOBBY CARDS WERE ISSUED FOR A 1922 AMERICAN RE-RELEASE UNDER THE TITLES THE INFERNO AND DANTE'S INFERNO BY JAWITZ PICTURES OF NEW YORK.

L'INFERNO

("The Inferno"; Francesco Bertolini, Adolfo Padovan & Giuseppe de Liguoro, 1911: Italy)

Based on Dante Alighieri's epic poem *La Divina Commedia*, and visually modelled after the illustrations for that text executed in 1857 by Gustave Doré, Milano Film's **L'Inferno** was the longest, most ambitious feature ever produced in Italy up to that point, and stands as the very first classic of Satanic cinema. It was also one of the first foreign feature-length films to be successfully distributed in the USA, where it was presented as **Dante's Inferno** by the Monopol Film Company, who issued the first ever 24-sheet movie poster to promote it. A dizzying guide through the realms of Purgatory and Hell, the film presents – in fifty-four separate *tableaux* – an array of demons, devils, fallen angels and naked, tormented sinners in beautiful vistas of unholy imagination. Torture, mutilation and cannibalism are just a few of the atrocities depicted, with victims who have been maimed, eviscerated, decapitated; one man is shown devouring another's head. Beasts such as Cerberus, the three-headed dog, are represented, less successfully, through crude puppet animation. Lucifer was played by Augusto Milla. Several episodes of the film were originally filmed and released in 1908, under the title **Saggi Dell'Inferno Dantesco** ("Scenes From Dante's Inferno"). Another **L'Inferno**, made in 1910 and released in 1911, was produced by Helios Film and directed by Giuseppe Berardi and Arturo Busnengo; this 18-minute vision, filled with nightmarish imagery, closes with incredible scenes

of a gigantic, cannibal Lucifer devouring the nude body of a human female he clutches in his fingertips (a scene recurring in Milano's version, minus the nudity). Also included was a sequence during which the historical figure of Francesca da Rimini may be glimpsed with bare breasts. It is generally accepted that Helios' **L'Inferno** was an opportunistic cash-in, made to capitalize on the advance publicity generated by Milano's high-profile production. Helios followed up with a sequel, **Il Purgatorio**, later in 1911, while Ambrosio Film also joined in the Satanic spree, reportedly producing their own **Il Purgatorio** that same year. Another Satanic film from Italy in 1911 was Aquila's **La Vendetta Di Satana** ("Satan's Revenge"). That year Ambrosio also produced **Le Tentazioni Di Sant'Antonio** ("The Temptations Of Saint Anthony"), the longest film version to date of Gustave Flaubert's hallucinatory novel, with vivid scenes of the tortured ascetic beleaguered by Satan's taloned she-devils who morph into writhing, semi-naked beauties. The final part of *La Divina Commedia* was filmed in 1912 by Psiche Films, under the title **Il Paradisio** (**Visioni Dantesche**) ("Paradise: Visions From Dante").

LE TENTAZIONI DI SANT'ANTONIO – PRODUCTION PHOTOGRAPH.

ONÉSIME AUX ENFERS - PRODUCTION PHOTOGRAPH.

ONÉSIME AUX ENFERS
("Onésime In Hell"; Jean Durand, 1912: France)

The more than fifty short slapstick movies starring Ernest Bourbon as Onésime, a dandefied *idiot savant*, stand not only as the best work by director Jean Durand – who also directed other series featuring characters Zigoto and Calino – but include some of the early classics of French cinema. In these films, Durand created a kind of hyper-realistic anarchy of objects, buildings, even time and space, in revolt; a radical logic of destruction and disorder verging on global chaos. To create such aberrations, Durand formed his own cine-troupe of extreme knockabout performers, Les Pouittes, who would heavily influence Mack Sennett in the creation of his own Keystone repertory crew.[1]

1. Les Pouittes included actor Gaston Modot, future "star" of Luis Buñuel's L'Âge D'Or, as well as stunt aviator Charles Nungesser, acrobat and animal-trainer Berthe Dagmar, and various comic actors.

SATANA
("Satan"; Luigi Maggi: 1912: Italy)

Inspired by Milton's *Paradise Lost*, this is a film about the Devil in two parts – *Il Gran Ribelle* ("The Great Rebellion") and *Il Distruttore* ("The Destroyer") – each comprising two acts. In the first act, *Satana Contro Il Creatore* ("Satan Versus The Creator"), we see Satan defeated by the angels and cast out of Heaven; he falls to earth where, in the form of a serpent, he causes hallucinations and violence amongst men. Devil-worship and the Tower of Babel are also featured. In the second act, *Satana Contro Il Salvatore* ("Satan Versus The Saviour"), Satan is seen in Jerusalem, trying in vain to prevent Christ from rising from the grave. In the third act, *Il Demone*

SATANA - PRODUCTION PHOTOGRAPH.

Verde, Ossia Satanai Nel Medioevo ("The Green Demon – Namely, Satan In The Middle Ages"), Satan gives an alchemist the power to make absinthe, causing mayhem amongst a conclave of monks. Satan, himself intoxicated by the green drink, contemplates corpses. Finally, in the fourth act – *Il Demone Rosso, Ossia Satanai Nella Vita Moderna* ("The Red Demon – Namely, Satan In Modern Times") – we move to the industrial age, where Satan foments a workers' uprising which results in death. The film is now regarded as lost, and only an 8-minute fragment has been located to date. It was produced by the prolific Società Anonima Ambrosio, who also released the two-reeler **Il Castello Del Diavolo** ("The Devil's Castle", 1913), in which a soldier rises in power by selling his soul to Satan, until his castle is burned to the ground. The Devil (played by Alfred de Manby) also appeared in much more modest British production, **The Tempter**, in 1913; in this short phantasy, the King of Hell boasts of his evil powers of temptation in three vignettes of cardinal sin, concerning a cheating husband (lust/adultery), a gambler (greed), and an alcoholic (gluttony). A diabolic pact was also at the heart of another UK film, **The Devil's Bondman** (1915, directed by Percy Nash), in which an ex-convict encounters a sinister Chinese magus (seemingly Satan in disguise) in an opium den and subsequently acquires the power to win fortunes at cards. This 3-reel film was released in the USA as **The Scorpion's Sting,** perhaps a reference to the climax of the story, in which the convict's life of crime is curtailed by a final visitation from the Devil, sending his speeding motor-car careering off the road with fatal results. Frank Wilson's **A Deal With The Devil** (Hepworth, 1916) was also a Faustian soul-selling phantasy, one of dozens produced in early global cinema.

SATANA

("Satan"; Abraham Kaminski, 1912: Russia/Poland)

Also known by its Yiddish title **Got, Mentsh Un Tayvl** ("God, Man And Devil"), this short interpretation of a play of that name written by Jacob Gordin in 1900 is the first Russian film to directly cite the King of Hell in its title (a good number of others would follow). Produced by Moïse Toubin's Sila ("Force") production house, which specialised in theatrical adaptations, **Satana** tells of a wager between Lucifer and God that a pious and religious man can be corrupted by money. Posing as the man's business partner, Lucifer engenders sufficient riches for the man to plunge into a life of avarice, lust and infidelity. A later version of Gordin's Faustian play was the American Yiddish-language film **Got, Mentsh, Un Tayvl**, directed in 1949 by Joseph Seiden, who produced a catalogue of movies for Jewish audiences.

El SATARIO

("The Satyr"; Anonymous, c.1912: Argentina)

Often alternatively credited as a 1920s Mexican or 1930s Cuban production (due to its "anti-religious" nature), the mythic stag movie **El Satario** is in any case probably the earliest example of "devilish" film pornography. A group of nude young women are frolicking in a field when they are accosted by a horned figure resembling a devil, who drags one of them away for a bout of fellatio, then copulates with the others. The film includes close-ups of vaginal penetration and other obscenities. Scholars believe the film may actually have been filmed outside Rosario, a city in Argentina, and that it may have been inspired by Diaghilev's ballet *L'Après-Midi D'Un Faune* ("Afternoon Of A Faun"), with Nijinsky as a nymph-chasing satyr, which scandalized Paris in 1912.

The DEVIL

(Reginald Barker & Thomas H. Ince, 1915: USA)

A moralistic film depicting Satan as a suave tempter leading an artist and a married woman into adultery, with predictably unhappy results; in the end, the lovers are condemned to Hell (depicted with Doré-style imagery). The film may be seen as reinforcing the stereotype of the "artistic" (creative and therefore morally weak) victim who easily succumbs to the Devil's will,[1] a plot device which would be repeated in films such as Harley Knoles' **The Devil's Toy** (1916, with Edwin Stevens as Satan) and Lois Weber's **Even As You And I** (1917), involving the temptations of alcohol and lust which are sent, in imp form, by Satan (here called Saturniska) to destroy a married couple. **The Temptations Of Satan** (1914) was an example of the Devil directly tempting a woman (women were also viewed as being easy prey for the hounds of Hell). In **The Devil's Darling**, also made in 1915, another woman contemplates selling her soul, but reconsiders when she sees a vision of tormented souls in Hell; the film includes a sacrificial chamber piled with human bones. Barker and Ince's **The Devil** was the third film based on Ferenc Molnár's play *Az Ördög*; there were several subsequent silent film interpretations of the work, including **Az Ördög**, a Hungarian production directed by Mihály Kertész in 1918; Theo Frenkel's Dutch production **De Duivel In Amsterdam** ("The Devil In Amsterdam", 1919); and **The Devil** (James Young, 1920), which starred original stage actor George Arliss.

1. One of the earliest films involving an artist selling his soul to Satan was a British production, The Devil's Bargain, directed by A.E. Coleby in 1908.

THE DEVIL'S DARLING - PRODUCTION PHOTOGRAPH.

THE DEVIL - SATAN AND VICTIM; PRODUCTION PHOTOGRAPH (*OPPOSITE PAGE*).

DER STUDENT VON PRAG – TWO DOUBLES MEET; FRAME
ENLARGEMENT.

Der STUDENT VON PRAG

("The Student Of Prague"; Stellan Rye, 1913: Germany)

A film adaptation, co-authored by the horror/occult novelist Hanns Heinz Ewers, of E.T.A.Hoffmann's short story *Sylvesternacht*, also drawing on elements of Hoffmann's novel *Die Elixiere Des Teufels* ("The Devil's Elixirs"). Produced by Deutsche Bioskop, the film deals with the occult myth of the *doppelgänger*, or double, and tells how a hedonistic student (played by Paul Wegener) sells his mirror reflection to a mysterious stranger in exchange for untold wealth. The stranger turns out to be Satan, and the student finally perishes at the homicidal hands of his own malevolent double. Filmed amid the twisting medieval streets of old Prague, **Der Student Von Prag** distils a wondrous alchemy of black magic, terror, and dark beauty. The cinematography was supervised by Guido Seeber, a German film pioneer who first experimented with moving images in the 1890s, and developed his own Seeberograph projection system. It was Seeber who in 1911 set up Bioskop's glass film studio in the marshes of Neubabelsberg, later expanded by UFA into Europe's largest production house. Stellan Rye's next film, **Die Augen Des Ole Brandis** ("The Eyes Of Ole Brandis", 1913) was again scripted by Hann Heinz Ewers and concerned a young man who obtains from a mysterious, hunch-backed antiquarian the means to see the reality of human nature; horrified by revelations of relentless avarice, lust, vanity and treachery, he is driven to the brink of insanity and suicide. Ewers and Rye collaborated again on **Die Eisbraut** ("The Ice Bride", 1913), from Ewers' novella

John Hamilton Llewellyns Ende ("The Death Of John Hamilton Llewellyn"), but the film was immediately banned by Berlin police because it contained scenes of nudity and lust for a frozen corpse. In 1914, Rye – who had reputedly come to Germany after being jailed for sodomy in his native Denmark – made his final film **Das Haus Ohne Tür** ("The House Without Doors", 1914, from a novel by Thea von Harbou),[1] in which he contrived sadistic imagery and hinted at the stylized, psychogeometric set designs that would feature five years later in Robert Wiene's **Das Cabinet Des Dr. Caligari**; he was killed in WWI in November 1914. E.T.A Hoffmann's *Die Elixiere Des Teufels* was also used as the basis for **Das Hexenlied** ("The Witch-Song", 1919), and was directly filmed in 1920 (an Austrian production with Rudolf Rudolfi as the Devil) and 1922 (in Germany). **Der Student Von Prag** was emulated soon after release in an abbreviated production by French company Gaumont, who released their own *doppelgänger* story **La Double Incarnation De William Sheep** ("The Double Incarnation Of William Sheep") in September 1913;[2] Deutsche Bioskop released **Der Andere Student Von Prag**, a 13-minute parody of their own film, in early 1914.

1. With Russian actor Vladimir Vasilyevich Maksimov; it was released in Russia by the Mystic Partnership as **Taverna Satany** ("Satan's Tavern").

2. Sheep falls asleep playing chess and dreams that a mysterious old man assumes his physical form in order to rape his wife; the film also includes some stop-motion animation of chess-pieces.

CRUEL, CRUEL LOVE
(Mack Sennett, 1914: USA)

Among the highlights from Charlie Chaplin's early Keystone comedies, **Cruel, Cruel Love** (released in March 1914) is notable for its closing sequence. Chaplin plays a jilted aristocrat who attempts suicide and has vivid visions of Hell, where he finds himself impaled on the pitch-forks of two horned devils. A Satanic figure also appears in Sennett's **Droppington's Devilish Deed** (1915), in which Droppington (Chester Conklin) is working as a theatre hand and witnesses a stage magician conjure up the Devil. The infernal ending of **Cruel, Cruel Love** would be echoed in several subsequent slapstick shorts, among them Mirthquake's **All Is Lost** (1923) starring Bobby Dunn, and the Larry Semon vehicle **The Dome Doctor** (1925), in which Semon plays a calamity-prone hairdresser who, at the film's climax, is dragged down into Hell by a demon.

ALL IS LOST - LOBBY CARD.

DOKTOR X - PRODUCTION PHOTOGRAPH (*ABOVE*).
DEN MYSTISKE FREMMEDE – PRODUCTION PHOTOGRAPH
(*OPPOSITE TOP*); ENHVER – PRODUCTION PHOTOGRAPH
(*OPPOSITE BOTTOM*).

DOKTOR X

("Doctor X"; Robert Dinesen, 1915: Denmark)

One of Denmark's first significant works of Satanic cinema was a variation on the Faust legend, in which a young doctor falls into temptation when his more worldly colleague offers him wealth and power over women. As usual in such tales, this path leads him to damnation and suicide. The film's bleak ending shows the colleague, now revealed as the figure of Mephistopheles, gloating over the doctor's corpse, his hand on the dead man's forehead in a gesture of possession. Dinesen's film was preceded by Holger-Madsen's 1914 production, **Den Mystiske Fremmede** ("The Mysterious Stranger"), which featured Alf Blütecher as Mefisto/Satan, who grants a man fame in exchange for a decade of his life. 1915 also saw the release of another film meditation on good and evil, Vilhelm Glückstadt's **Enhver** ("Anybody"), based on a play by Hugo von Hofmannsthal. With demonic and skeletal figures (Satan and Death), and special effects camera tricks to depict doubling, **Enhver** is a classic phantasy of early Danish cinema. Another Faust variation from 1915 was the UK production **The Devil To Pay**, directed by Edwin J. Collins for Martin, a company who specialized in comedy but made occasional dramatic films such as **For East Is East** (1913, released in the USA as **In The Python's Den**), about a sadistic prince in India who feeds his rivals to snakes.

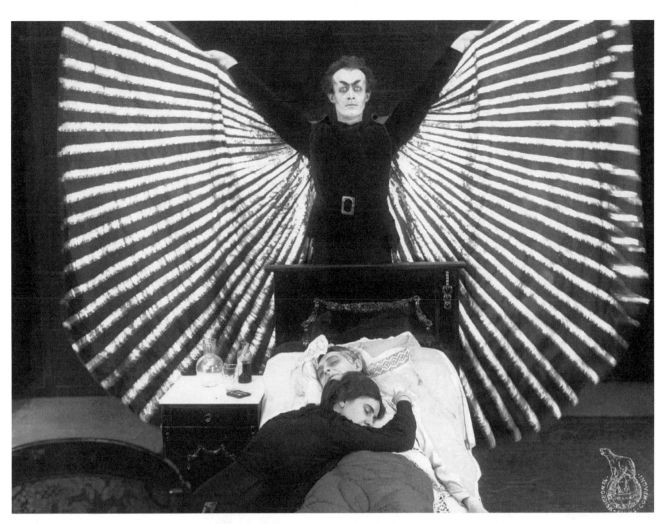

The MAGIC SKIN

(Richard Ridgely, 1915: USA)

This Edison production is an adaptation of Honoré de Balzac's story "La Peau De Chagrin", which concerns a young musician falling foul of a sexual vamp in Paris. When he visits an antique shop to buy her a necklace, the shop's proprietor reveals himself as the Devil. He offers the musician a trade; his soul in exchange for a "magic skin" which will fulfil his evey desire. Problems arise when the skin shrinks after each wish, dragging the young man's health down with it; in the end the sadistic vamp deserts him, the good-hearted girl who loves him kills herself, the skin completely vanishes, and he finds himself in Hell. As in (too) many horror films, this brush with Beelzebub turns out to have been just a warning dream, which sets the artist's head straight so he can marry the righteous girl and spurn the sexual wanton, who – like all of her kind – is now revealed as nothing but an infernal concubine. The very first version of Balzac's story was Albert Capellani's **La Peau De Chagrin** ("The Skin Of Misery", 1909); later adaptations include **Desire** (1920), **The Dream Cheater** (1920), **Narayana** (1920), and **Slave Of Desire** (1923).

THE MAGIC SKIN - PRODUCTION PHOTOGRAPH.

RAPSODIA SATANICA
("Satanic Rhapsody"; Nino Oxilia, 1915: Italy)

A Satanic melodrama from Cines – filmed and previewed in 1915 but held back from release until 1917 – in which Mephisto (played by Ugo Bazzini) grants an ageing countess (played by Lyda Borelli) eternal youth in exchange for her soul. When she breaks the pact, she ages rapidly and collapses in death. With a special musical score by leading composer Pietro Mascagni, **Rapsodia Satanica** was one of the most lavish film productions of its era. Borelli was the *prima diva* of Italian cinema, the accentuation of her physical appearance and gestures, often in close-up, making her an important early movie star. Borelli's other key *diva* role of 1915 was in Carmine Gallone's **Fior Di Male** ("Flower Of Evil"), a sensational Cines production of murder and prostitution which also featured actresses Pina Menichelli and Fulvia Perini. By the time of **Rapsodia Satanica**'s dispute-delayed release in 1917, she had also played the lead role in another dark melodrama, Carmine Gallone's **Malombra** (1916), a gothic murder-suicide tale set in an ancient castle, based on the 1881 novel by Antonio Fogazzaro. In Gallone's **La Falena** ("The Moth"), also made in 1916, Borelli – playing a fatally ill woman – made one of the screen's most exorbitant *diva* gestures, stripping naked in front of a crowd of guests before committing suicide.

The BLACK CROOK
(Robert G. Vignola, 1916: USA)

One of the earliest examples of the "Satanic pact" film, starring E.P. Sullivan as a criminal who must provide the Devil with fresh souls or be consigned to Hell himself. He eventually fails, and is consumed by the Inferno. Also in 1916, Edward Sloman – who the previous year had played Mephistopheles in Lubin's **Faust** – appeared as the Devil in his own **Sold To Satan**, granting eternal youth and wealth in exchange for human souls. The Devil also appeared in George Loane Tucker's 5-part pulp crime thriller **Sons Of Satan** (1915, released 1916), depicted as a leering mentor to the film's detective-turned-criminal-mastermind, and also in **The Master Smiles** (1916), again gloating over the follies and sins of mortals. **White Roses** (1914) was one of the first films in which Satan was depicted as an incarnation of wicked temptations (played by Harry Carter as Evil Thought), a device which would become familiar in numerous animated cartoons in which characters are torn between the exhortations of an angel on one shoulder and a devil on the other. The Devil, or Mephistopheles, was played by Albert Morrison in **Faust**, a 1916 production by the California Motion

Picture Corporation; the film was abandoned before completion due to rising costs, but footage from it later turned up in George Terwilliger's **The Eternal Mephisto** (1919, also known as **The Price Woman Pays**).

THE DEVIL'S BONDWOMAN - PRODUCTION PHOTOGRAPH (*ABOVE*).

CONSCIENCE - PRODUCTION PHOTOGRAPH (*OVERLEAF, TOP*).

The DEVIL'S BONDWOMAN
(Lloyd B. Carleton, 1916: USA)

Adele Farrington plays a sex-crazed vamp whose carnal depravities are so intense that they catch the eye of Satan himself, who eventually carries her back to Hell and seduces her in human form. An unusual inclusion of the supernatural in the vamp genre, used to underscore the opinion that sexually aggressive women were nothing less than the concubines of the Devil on earth. Another film to attribute the vamp with more than earthly powers was Bertram Bracken's **Conscience**, released the following year, in which Serama, Satan's royal consort, is cast out of Paradise and reincarnates on earth as a vamp named Ruth, whose mysterious companion turns out to be the Devil himself. She proceeds to run riot, destroying a succession of men and driving several of them to suicide; finally, this wanton succubus is put on trial in a court of the angel Conscience, where the demons Avarice, Lust, Vanity and Hate all testify to her evil doings. She is sentenced to live forever with the memories of her sins. Scenes of damned souls in Hell are notable for displaying full male and female nudity, with only the genital area strategically covered. The role of Serama – originally intended for Theda Bara – was taken by Gladys Brockwell, who joined other vamps of the period such as Alice Hollister, who appeared in Robert G. Vignola's **The Vampire** (1913) and **The Destroyer** (1915). Of all the US films made in the 1910s which offer cinematic visions of Hell, Harry A. Pollard's **The Devil's Assistant** (also 1917) boasts perhaps the most imaginative and arresting scenario. The film revolves around an experimental drug, which a doctor invents in order to force a woman to succumb to his lust. As she eventually lies dying, she is haunted by scenes from the underworld, including devils and demons, the ferryman of the dead, and Cerberus, the three-headed Hell-hound.

PREFERISCO L'INFERNO
("I Prefer Hell"; Eleuterio Rodolfi, 1916: Italy)

A satirical vision of Hell from Rodlfi, who also takes the lead role as a man who accidentally falls into Satan's underworld mansions. Satan sets him free, on condition that he takes His demon son, Asmodeus, with him to show him the ways of humankind. Both man and demon soon become bewildered, and decide they prefer life in Hell. Satan rewards Rodolfi by turning Asmodeus into a young woman (played by comedienne Gigetta). A diabolic Ambrosio production, acclaimed for its art direction and cinematography.

SHADOWED BY THE DEVIL
(Unique Film Co., 1916: USA)

The extremely short-lived Unique was one of America's first "race film" producers, creating films with all-negro players, for all-negro audiences. **Shadowed By The Devil**, a morality play featuring a man possessed by Satan, stands as perhaps the first black horror movie, although details of its plot are scarce.

DEVILED CRABS

(Jaxon Comedies, 1917: USA)

A Pokes and Jabbs slapstick comedy from Vim Comedy of Florida, one of hundreds of 2-reel shorts made by the company between 1915 and 1917. This particular episode crosses into Satanic territory when the unemployed Pokes, after gorging on beer and devilled crabs, has a feverish vision of the Devil with Jabbs' face. Pokes signs a diabolic pact exchanging his soul for riches; when he tries to escape from Jabbs/Satan, he finds himself trapped in a burning haystack – only to wake up with his feet in the fire, realizing it was all a spice-and-alcohol-induced nightmare. Released the same year as **Deviled Crabs** was a Joker comedy from Universal entitled **What The ——?**, in which a man dreams of descending into Hades and claiming Satan's throne; the film starred Milburn Moranti as Satan, and Lillian Peacock as the Queen of Hell. Another Satanic comedy was Reelcraft's **A Simp And Satan** (1920), in which the Devil drags an engaged couple into the bowels of Hell in order to show them the horrors that await them in married life, with the woman revealed as an adulterous "vampire".

Die MEMOIREN DES SATANS

("The Memoirs Of Satan"; Robert Heymann, 1917-18: Germany)

The Devil is invoked yet again, played by Kurt Brenkendorf, in Luna-Film's **Die Memoiren Des Satans**, a 4-part serial based on the 1825 satirical novel by Wilhelm Hauff. The 2-part novel – basically an autobiography of Satan on Earth – was rendered in 4 filmic parts: **Doktor Mors** (1917), **Fanatiker Des Lebens** ("Fanatic Of

DIE DAME, DER TEUFEL, UND DIE PROBIERMAMSELL - NIGHTCLUB IN HELL; PRODUCTION PHOTOGRAPH.

Life", 1917), **Der Fluchbeladene** ("The Accursed", 1917), and **Der Sturz Der Menschheit** ("The Fall Of Mankind", 1918). The figure of Satan (played by actor Alfred Abel) also appeared in Rudolf Biebrach's **Die Dame, Der Teufel Und Die Probiermamsell** ("The Lady, The Devil And The Fashion Model", 1918, scripted by Robert Wiene), which includes scenes in Hell.

SATANA LIKUYUSHCHIY

("Satana Exultant"; Yakov Protazanov, 1917: Russia)

The primary Satanic film to emerge from Russia during the silent era, although there were numerous others. Two brothers, a priest and a hunchbacked painter, are visited by a mysterious stranger (the Devil, or his agent, played by Aleksandr Chabrov), who tempts the minister (played by Ivan Mozzhukhin) with whispers of carnal desire; the end result is an adulterous affair with his sister-in-law, who later gives birth to an illegitimate child. The preacher is finally killed when his church collapses. When the bastard boy (also played by Mozzhukhin) grows up, he is in turn ensnared by the Devil, resulting in a swathe of shocking debauchery. Another infernal Russian film of 1917 was Vyacheslav Viskovsky's "mystical drama" **Venchal Ikh Satana** ("Married By Satan"), adapted from the 1903 novel *Adskiye Chary* ("Hell's Delights") by V.I. Kryzhanovskaya-Rochester;[1] the plot involves the Devil controlling human affairs, and the advertising poster – by artist Georgiy Alekseyev – which survives is a minor masterpiece of erotic horror combining demons, skulls, candles, and a nude girl being taloned by a rabid black cat. Russia's crowning Satanic work of the decade was Aleksandr Sanin's **Devy Gory** ("Mountain Virgin", 1918), also known as **Legenda Ob Antikhriste** ("Legend Of The Anti-Christ"), in which Satan and Judas Iscariot scour the earth for virgin souls in a metaphysical fusion of mysticism and sensuality. When Russian film-makers absconded to France after the Revolution, Satanic traces came with them – a French film also shot in 1919, Iosif Yermoliev's Ermolieff-Films' **La Nuit Du 11 Septembre**, was banned from exhibition until 1922 due to "blasphemous" scenes of a semi-nude woman (Russian actress Eugenia Boldirev) being crucified. Yermoliev – who also produced **Satana Likuyushchiy** – was at the forefront of the Russian film-makers who fled their homeland to relocate in Paris, having worked with Pathé's Russian branch for a number of years.

1. Vera Ivanovna Kryzhanovskaya was a devotee of occultism; she worked as a spirit medium, was married to a fellow spiritualist, and claimed that her numerous occult-flavoured novels were dictated to her by

VENCHAL IKH SATANA - FILM POSTER ART BY GEORGIY
ALEKSEYEV.

the ghost of the English poet John Wilmot, Earl of Rochester (best known for the epic pornographic work *Sodom*, published in 1684, in which a royal proclamation authorising a program of mass homosexual buggery leads the kingdom's women to amuse themselves with dildoes and sex with dogs). Other films derived from Kryzhanovskaya's novels include Viktor Turzhanskiy's **Ray Bez Adama** ("Paradise Without Adam") and its sequel, **Obmanutaya Yeva** ("The Deception Of Eve"), both released in 1918.

2. 2. Georgiy Alekseyev began as a writer and illustrator of children's books, such as *Volshebnyy Karlik Krosha* ("Krosha, The Magic Dwarf"); he also created monumental tombstones, and after the Russian Revolution he worked as a sculptor and created many monuments to the Communist ideal, including the well-known relief *Soyuz Rabochikh I Krestyan* ("Union Of Workers And Peasants"), which still survives on the wall of the State Historical Museum, and a famous statue of Lenin.

ч. 1 МЕЧТА ЛЮБВИ-БЕЗУМНЫЙ СОНЬ. ч. 2 НѢТЪ ДРУЖБЫ БЕЗЪ ОБМАНА.
ч. 3 ШКВАЛЪ СТРАСТИ ч. 4 ИДІОТЪ. ч. 5 ПОХОРОННЫЙ МАРШЪ ДЬЯВОЛА.
УЧАСТВ. М. М. ГОРИЧЕВА, П. В. КОЗМОВСКАЯ,
О. Г. ГЛАДКОВА, А. И. НАЗАРОВА.
СНЯТО ВЪ КРЫМУ, КУРОРТЪ „ГУРЗУФЪ"
АКЦ. ОБЩ. „БІОФИЛЬМЪ" ПЕТРОГРАДЪ – МОСКВА – ЕКАТЕРИНБУРГЪ.

SKERTSO DYAVOLA - FILM POSTER BY IRO-L (*OPPOSITE*).

SKERTSO DYAVOLA
("The Devil's Scherzo"; Viktor Turzhanskiy, 1917: Russia)

Russia's psycho-salon genre finally achieved sensory overload in this demonic production, whose promotional poster amply illustrates its theme of human puppets battered and torn apart by evil forces, literally dancing to the Devil's tune. The film's hero is a "Satanic master" bent on the manipulation and destruction of all around him; this devotee of Hell seduces a female friend of his wife and forces his wife to fornicate with another man, driving her to the lunatic asylum, then causes his lover to kill herself. He then goads his son, a congenital idiot, into raping his daughter (the imbecile's sister), leading them on the path to to death. The film ends with the man exultant, hailing the Devil as he stands knee-deep in the corpses of those he has murdered.

SATAN ON EARTH
(Gaumont, 1918-19: USA)

Initially announced as a feature depicting the Devil's attempts to wreak evil throughout the ages of mankind from ancient Rome to the present-day, **Satan On Earth** had, by its release, been reduced to a mere two reels. The film, described by producers Gaumont as a "photo-novelty", reportedly began with the fall of Lucifer. Promotional posters and ads were created, but the film may have been quickly withdrawn after its obscure initial opening in Flushing, Long Island – presumably after negative audience reaction or through fear of controversy. Existing production photos show Satan as a ragged, horned figure hounded by an archangel.

TO HELL WITH THE KAISER - PRODUCTION PHOTOGRAPH.

TO HELL WITH THE KAISER
(George Irving, 1918: USA)

When America belatedly entered WWI, the first wave of propaganda demonizing their enemy, Kaiser Wilhelm, was headed by this film in which he is accused of signing a pact with Satan. After he is seen brutally raping an American girl in a church, the Kaiser is captured by US forces and commits suicide, only for his soul to fly straight to Hell. In the film's final twist, Satan (played by Walter P. Lewis) acknowledges the new arrival's superior capacity for evil, and hands him His infernal throne. Poster images showed Wilhelm as an octopus with a human head, as part of what was possibly the first ever film example of Satan used as a political propaganda tool. The Kaiser was also shown as an ally of the Devil, and enemy of Christ, in Howard Gaye's **Restitution** from the same year;[1] and in Rupert Julian's **The Kaiser, The Beast Of Berlin** (also 1918), he was portrayed as greedy, disliked by his own troops, and finally too weak to resist the USA.

1. Produced by Mena Film Company, **Restitution** was one of numerous films which attempted to depict the malign influence of Satan throughout the ages; scenes included the Garden of Eden and ancient Rome, with the crucifixion of Christ and Nero's torture-atrocities against the Christian scum. Alfred Garcia played Satan. Another 1918 film with a depiction of Satan was the German production **Hiob** ("Job"), with Hans Adalbert Schlettow in the infernal role.

BLADE AF SATANS BOG - PRODUCTION PHOTOGRAPHS
(*ABOVE & OPPOSITE*).

BLADE AF SATANS BOG

("Pages From Satan's Book"; Carl Theodor Dreyer, 1919: Denmark)

Blade Af Satans Bog (released in Denmark in 1921) depicts the malefic influence of Satan on human affairs throughout the ages. This is shown in a series of chronological episodes, going back to the betrayal and crucifixion of Christ, then on to Spain and the Inquisition, then later to revolutionary France, and finally to then-contemporary Russia, with a Rasputin-like figure. Helge Nissen plays Satan, but the film is short on demonic revelry. Dreyer's next film of religious import would be **La Passion De Jeanne D'Arc** ("The Passion Of Jeanne D'Arc", 1927), a depiction of the interrogation, torture, trial and execution of the young girl who in the 15th century, inspired by religious visions, led the French army to victories against the English, but was eventually captured and accused of heresy. Dreyer's film, ground-breaking in its use of harsh lighting, minimal make-up, subterranean camera-angles and monumental close-ups – designed to accentuate the grotesque horror of Jeanne's ecclesiastical inquisitors – provoked the antipathy of the French church, who made severe cuts to Dreyer's final version without his consent. Dreyer's own negative was, like Jeanne, destroyed in a fire, and his definitive vision believed forever lost until, several decades later, a single surviving copy was located languishing in the bowels of a Norwegian lunatic asylum.

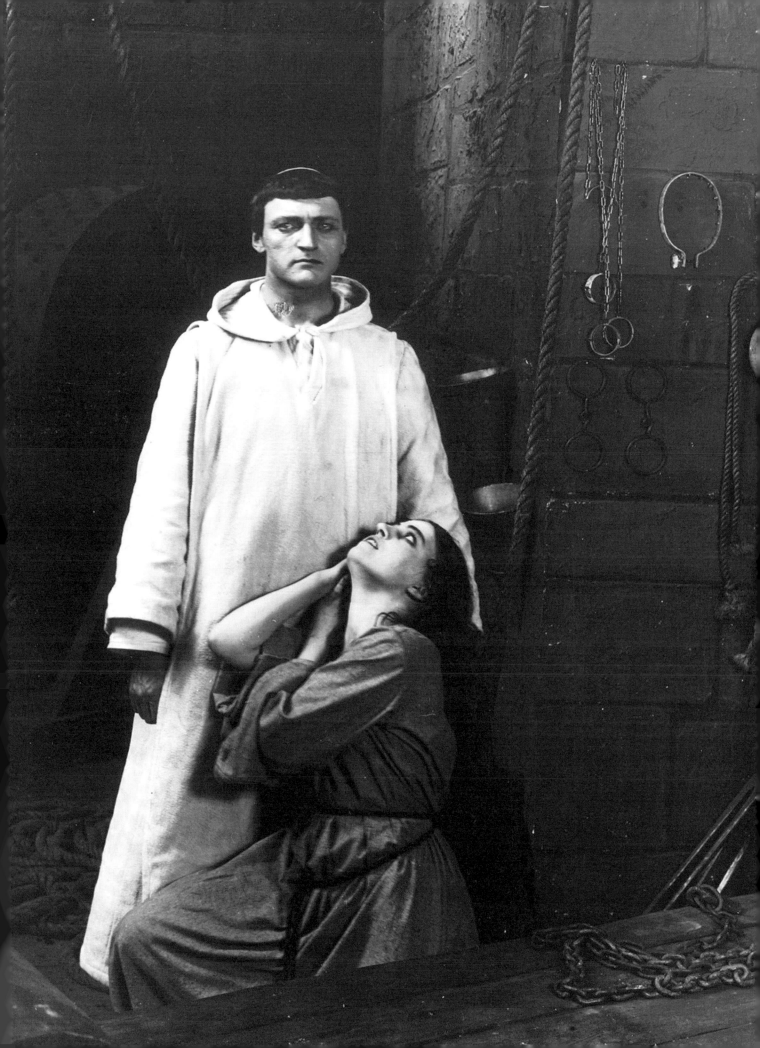

SATANAS

("Satan"; F. W. Murnau, 1919: Germany)

Another lost film which, like Howard Gaye's **Restitution**, Carl Dreyer's **Blade Af Satans Bog** and others, showed the baleful influence of Lucifer throughout human history. **Satanas** was divided into three time-frames – the first episode, set in ancient Egypt, featured the fallen angel as a destroyer, crushing mortals underfoot; the next showed an incestuous affair between the 15th-century orgiast Lucretia Borgia and her own son; and the final segment was set in then-contemporary Russia, where a Bolshevik leader goes mad with power and bloody slaughters.[1] Conrad Veidt, leading icon of the German silent cinema of the supernatural, played Lucifer – as he did in **Der Nicht Vom Weibe Geborene** and Richard Oswald's **Kurfürstendamm** (1920) – whilst photography was by the great Karl Freund. In Josef Stein's **Lucifer** (1922), the title role was played by Georg Heinrich Schnell. The Bulgarian director Vassil Gendov's **Dyavolat V Sofiya** ("The Devil In Sofia", 1921) is similar to **Kurfürstendamm**, and shows a bored Satan (Gendov) coming to earth, shacking up

DER TEUFEL UND DIE CIRCE - FILM POSTER BY JOSEF FENNEKER.

with a prostitute, and sampling human city life; he soon realises Hell is far preferable. A ubiquitous figure in Teutonic cinema of this period, Satan was also depicted in Edmund Linke's **Satan Diktator** (1920, played by Willy Engst), in **Wie Satan Starb** ("The Death Of Satan", 1920), directed by Otto Rippert and Heinz Hanus, and in Adolf Gärtner's **Der Teufel Und Die Circe** ("The Devil And The Siren", 1921, played by Walter von Allwoerden). And Satan soon appeared again in **Der Mann, Der Das Lachen Verlernte** ("The Man Who Forgot How To Laugh", 1922), an Austrian production directed by Richard Arvay and Norbert Garay.

1. This final part marks **Satanas** as an early example of the German anti-Bolshevik cinema which would be exemplified a year later by Joseph Delmont's **Die Entfesselte Menschheit** ("Humanity Unleashed"), in which a Bolshevik fanatic plunges his country into a holocaust of civil war, disease and internecine slaughter. Anti-Bolshevism was established in Germany in 1918 with the formation of the Antibolschewistische Liga.

Die TEUFELSKIRCHE
("The Devil's Church"; Hans Mierendorff, 1919: Germany)
Paul Rehkopf plays the Devil in this oneiric film conflagration, couched as a nightmare, in which Satan comes to a small village after its church mysteriously burns down. When a local farmer refuses to give up his land for a new church, the horned one burns down his house whilst seducing his wife (played by Agnes Straub with breasts bursting from her bodice) in an notably erotic sequence. Lust, greed, temptation and evil run riot as the Devil builds His church on Earth.

Die GEBURT DES ANTICHRIST
("The Birth Of The Anti-Christ"; Fritz Fehér, 1921: Austria)
From Fehér, a purveyor of twisted, expressionistic cinema who also appeared as an actor in **Das Cabinet Des Dr. Caligari**, came the first film phantasy of the Beast 666, created some fifty years before more famous elaborations such as **The Omen**. Framed not as a supernatural phenomenon but more as a descent into insanity, Fehér's tale is that of an artist who was sent to prison for killing a church-robber, and marries upon his release. When he discovers that his wife is a fallen nun, he starts to believe that his newly-born son is the Anti-Christ, and that he must deliver mankind from

DIE GEBURT DES ANTICHRIST – PRODUCTION PHOTOGRAPHS *(ABOVE RIGHT & OVERLEAF VERSO)*.

its clutches. After various attempts to kill the infant fail, his wife has him committed to a lunatic asylum. The artist manages to escape and launch one final homicidal attack upon the child, but is shot dead by his pursuers. Although the film is believed lost, contemporary reviews suggest that Fehér created a suitably nightmarish environment in which to convey this dark spiral of religious mania, madness and death.

HÄXAN – PRODUCTION PHOTOGRAPH.

HÄXAN
("Witch"; Benjamin Christensen, 1921-22: Sweden)

After directing four films in Denmark between 1914 and 1921, Christensen chose Swedish company Svensk Filmindustri to produce his next project, a film inspired by the texts and images which emanated from the European witchcraft holocaust of the Middle Ages. The result, **Häxan**, was not only his materpiece, but a seminal milestone in the history of global cinema which remains unsurpassed in its nightmarish visions and depictions of psychopathic perversion. After studying the 1487 witch-hunter's bible *Malleus Maleficarum* ("Hammer Of The Witches"), Christensen set out to expose its core matter – the way in which medieval superstition explained away physical and mental illness as witchcraft, particularly in women. Drawing on the book's vivid descriptions of tortures and inquisition, the director also evoked the many panoramas of weird horror to be found in witchcraft and demonolatry paintings by artists such as Francken, Brueghel, Goya, Grien, Teniers, Rosa, and

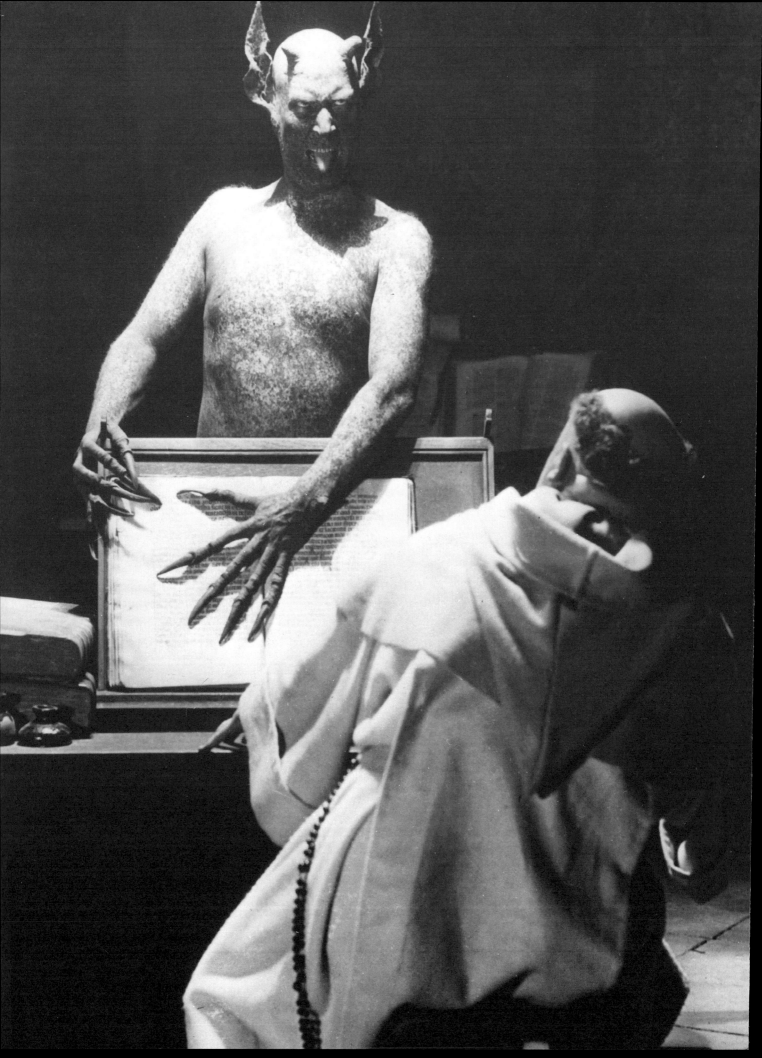

HÄXAN – PRODUCTION PHOTOGRAPHS (*ABOVE, OPPOSITE &*
FOLLOWING PAGES).

others – scenes of naked midnight black magic orgies, scattered skulls and bones, skeletal beasts, corpses, infant sacrifice and hellish monstrosities, all presided over by the horned, leering and priapic figure of Satan (played in the film by Christensen himself). Against these scenes of unbridled malevolence, **Häxan** shows the response of the clergy – systematic torture, imprisonment and sexual degradation. The film is arranged in seven chapters, beginning with a history of cosmological belief systems which culminates with Hell, the Devil and the witches' Sabbat, illustrated by various paintings and a mechanical diorama. The second chapter, set in 1488, begins by depicting an old hunchbacked witch at work, concocting potions from such ingredients as human bones, snakes, frogs, and rotting body parts culled from a gallows corpse; another brew is an aphrodisiac made from boiled cat faeces and dove hearts. Also shown are two anatomists accused of witchcraft after procuring a female corpse for dissection, followed by the film's first live manifestation of Satan (lasciviously incarnated by director Christensen), whose nocturnal tricks include inducing a nude woman to walk in her sleep, seducing another, and transporting an old hag to a "dream castle", where she sees cavorting pigs and other weird sights; this sequence is marked by trick photography including double exposures, backwards footage, and stop-motion animation (including a tiny animated demon). The next three chapters form a continuing story of the inquisitor monks, beginning with a mendicant hag accused of witchcraft, apprehended, and subjected to cruel tortures.

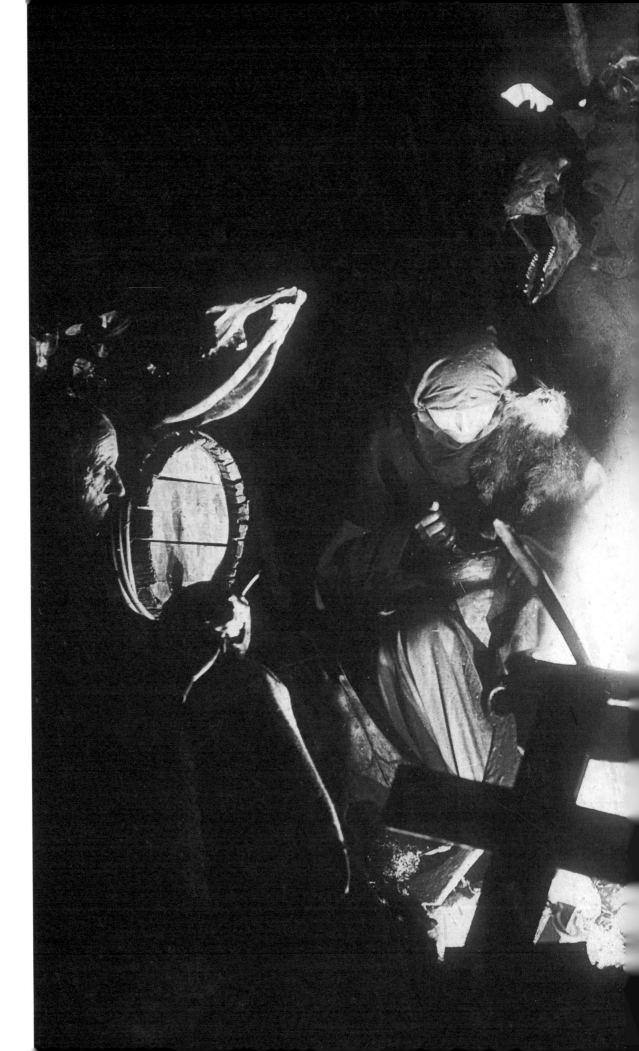

Her subsequent confessions, a string of lurid fantasies, are depicted by Christensen in the film's central sequences. They include scenes of giving birth to a human-devil hybrid, a hallucinatory sequence of witches flying to the Sabbat on broomsticks (after being doused with an unguent of animal fat and psychotropic plant extract), and then the Sabbat itself – cavorting devils and demons, a skeleton-horse, women beaten with sticks, witches spitting upon and trampling the cross, the ritual slaughter and cooking of a human baby, and a procession of witches kissing the Devil's foul, feculent anus. All of the women named and accused of witchcraft in the old hag's confessions are then arrested, and the viral process continues. The chapter ends with one of the monks, plagued by sexual fantasies of a young woman, accusing her of bewitching him; after he is brutally scourged, the girl is arrested and tortured. When she refuses to confess, the monks cruelly trick her into incriminating herself, showing how all those apprehended by the inquisitors are irrevocably doomed. Chaper Six opens by showing types of confession, ranging from the "insane" – a woman claims to have transformed into a cat to defecate on the holy altar whilst two human pigs stood guard – to the more mundane (tying knots to provoke abortions); Christensen then examines the various torture instruments used to extract such admissions – pincers, screws, hammers, chains, winches, wheels, spikes, rods, fire. The chapter ends with a subject first broached by Georges Méliès some twenty years previously in **Le Diable Au Convent**, that of possessed nuns. As in Méliès' short film, Satan is at large in a convent where the nuns, terrified of impure thoughts, regularly chastise themselves with spiked cinctures; when one sister is compelled by Satan to desecrate the Host and steal from the holy altar, the other nuns are driven into a hysterical frenzy. **Häxan** concludes with a reflective chapter set in modern times, where some of the conditions which caused women to be condemned as witches are examined. First, physical deformity – we see a dwarfish hunchback, an old woman with neurological disease, an old woman blind in one eye – and second, psychological disorders such as somnambulism, pyromania, sexual obsession, and kleptomania, afflictions which Christensen brackets as hysteria. Flashbacks to the 15th century include a partially nude woman being pricked with needles in order to find the "Devil's mark", an area of the back immune to sensation. The film ends with a still shot of three witches burning alive at the stake. **Häxan** was re-released in 1941, with an added filmed introduction in which Christensen explained some of the film's themes.

1. In 1968, **Häxan** was acquired for distribution by Antony Balch, an English film entrepreneur who since 1963 had been a specialist in exploitation cinema. As was his habit, Balch retitled the film, calling it **Witchcraft Through The Ages**; he also added a soundtrack composed of a jazz score by Daniel Humair and a commentary by his friend, the author William S. Burroughs. At that time Burroughs had just written and published a series of experimental novels – including *Naked Lunch*, *Soft Machine*, and *Nova Express* – which still represent the very pinnacle of American literature. Although the retroactive overdubbing of silent films is an abomination, it was fitting, at least, that one of the world's crowning cinematic works should be narrated by the world's leading literary innovator.

PAN TWARDOWSKI
("Lord Twardowski"; Wiktor Bieganski, 1921: Poland)

One of the earliest films from Poland to deal with the supernatural, **Pan Twardowski** is a variation on the Faust myth, deriving from an old Polish folk legend and set in the 16th century. The film contains scenes of nymphs and satyrs, the Devil (played by actor Stanisław Brylinski), a witches' Sabbat, the demon Beelzebub and his legions, and other supernatural manifestations. Another, less phantastic Polish interpretation of **Pan Twardowski** was filmed in 1936, by director Henryka Szaro, while **Pan Tvardovskiy** (1917) was the first version, adapted from Józef Ignacy Kraszewski's 1840 novel of the same name, and directed in Russia by Wladislaw Starewicz.

PAN TWARDOWSKI – WITCHES' SABBAT; PRODUCTION PHOTOGRAPH.

VESZÉLYBEN A POKOL – PRODUCTION PHOTOGRAPHS.

VESZÉLYBEN A POKOL
("Hell In Danger"; Béla Balogh, 1921: Hungary)
One of several films from this period in which Satan visits the world of mankind to interact with humans – often of the female kind. In this Star-Film fantasy, where Hell is depicted as a vast factory of punishments to be meted out, the Devil forfeits his power – symbolized by the loss of his horns – after kissing a virgin. He must now seduce and marry another woman, a slut who will betray him, to regain his infernal status. The film includes silhouette female nudity. When **Veszélyben A Pokol** was eventually released in Germany in 1925, by Continent-Film of Berlin under the title **Launen Des Satans** ("The Caprices Of Satan", 1925), it reportedly caused considerable consternation aming the film censors due to its depiction of cruel sexual manipulations and an apparent attack on the sanctity of marriage. Its female star, Vilma Bánky, had by that time moved to Hollywood and was starring in a succession of major studio productions.

DON JUAN ET FAUST – PRODUCTION PHOTOGRAPHS.

DON JUAN ET FAUST

("Don Juan And Faust'; Marcel L'Herbier, 1922: France)

L'Herbier was a film director for Gaumont whose experimental and intellectual leanings finally caused a rupture with the company, resulting in this, his final film for them, being released in a reportedly mangled form. **Don Juan Et Faust** was based on the pessimistic 1828 play by Christian Dietrich Garbbe in which Mephisopheles pits the alchemist against the great seducer, with a young woman's love as the prize. In the story's nihilistic climax Faust kills her, destroying his own life in the process, and Don Juan is dragged into Hell. L'Herbier's film remains notable for its avantgarde decor and costumes (by Claude Autant-Lara) and its orgy scenes, complete with bare-breasted females, which fell foul of the French censor. L'Herbier went on to form his own production company, Cinégraphic, which would allow his artistic experiments full and unfettered expression.

1. The legend of Don Juan, a fictional Spanish libertine and despoiler, dates back to the 17th century. In Tirso de Molina's 1630 play *El Burlador De Sevilla Y Convidado De Piedra* ("The Trickster Of Seville And The Stone Guest"), Don Juan is also attributed with semi-demonic powers. **Don Juan Tenorio** (1898), a short film based on the same-named 1844 play by José Zorrilla, stands among the very first cinematic works to emerge from Spain. Other early portrayals of Don Juan were produced in numerous countries, notably Victorin-Hippolyte Jasset's 1911 Éclair production **La Fin De Don Juan** ("Don Juan's Demise"), which ends with a spectral avenger compelling the seducer to descend into the underworld.

FAUST (1922) – PRODUCTION PHOTOGRAPH.

FAUST
(Gérard Bourgeois, 1922: France)
Mephisto in 3-D, shot using the Parolini process. The first Parolini 3-D film was **Rêve D'Opium** ("Opium Dream", 1921), and this was soon followed by **Faust**, starring veteran Georges Wague as Mephistopheles. Director Stéphane Passet used 3-D again in 1925 when filming **La Damnation De Faust**, another version of the enduring legend.

MY FRIEND THE DEVIL
(Harry Millarde, 1922: USA)
This Fox production is only interesting for its Satanic marketing, with posters showing the Devil luring a victim into temptation. The film's plot revolves around a doctor succumbing to such urgings and reading his dead wife's diary; what he finds changes his life forever. The film is based upon Georges Ohnet's 1889 novel *Le Docteur Rameau*, first adapted for screen as **Dr. Rameau** in 1915.

MY FRIEND THE DEVIL – FILM POSTER (*OPPOSITE PAGE*).

"Read her diary!"

WILLIAM FOX presents

MY FRIEND THE DEVIL

Adapted from Georges Ohnet's novel "DOCTOR RAMEAU"
SCENARIO BY PAUL H. SLOANE
DIRECTED BY
HARRY MILLARDE

THE PURITAN PASSIONS – PRODUCTION PHOTOGRAPH.

The PURITAN PASSIONS
(Frank Tuttle, 1923: USA)

A sinister version of Nathaniel Hawthorne's story "Feathertop", set in the time of the Salem witch trials, as a sorceress brings a scarecrow to life as part of her diabolical revenge on the judge who was once her lover. In Tuttle's film (by way of Percy MacKaye's 1908 play, *The Scarecrow*) Satan himself, rather than a witch, is the supernatural agent who breathes life into the scarecrow, giving the story a Faustian twist. This silent film has some genuinely horrific scenes, such as a Witches' Sabbat attended by misshapen night-crawlers, and the moment when the heroine glances at her lover, Lord Ravensbane, in the Mirror of Truth and sees him reflected as the grotesque and ragged scarecrow he really is. The earliest version of Hawthorne's story was **Lord Feathertop** (Edison, 1908), and one of the most notable was **Feathertop** (1913), a 1-reeler produced in colour by the Kinemacolor Company. Scarecrow magic also featured in Thannhauser's witchcraft fable **The Woman Who Did Not Care** (1913).

DANTE'S INFERNO – PRODUCTION PHOTOGRAPHS (*ABOVE &
FOLLOWING PAGES*).

DANTE'S INFERNO
(Henry Otto, 1924: USA)

Produced by William Fox, this morality tale of a ruthless businessman who finds redemption evokes the horrors of Hell to impart its message, horrors that churn in a nightmare caused by reading a "cursed" copy of Dante Alighieri's *Inferno* illustrated by Gustave Doré. Based on Francesco Bertolini's 1911 vision of Dante, and played out against huge painted backdrops, Otto's Hell is populated by sadistic demons and naked female sinners whose erogenous zones are concealed only by their long tresses, if at all. The film's iconic image is of actress Pauline Starke, shackled nude to a crag, being whipped by a huge, muscular demon. Hideous beasts and tortures are also shown, although not to the extremes conjured by Bertolini, and the whole nightmare is orchestrated by a gloating, demonic emissary of Lucifer (played by Robert Klein). Fox Corporation repeated the nightmare sequence trick two years later in **Hell's Four Hundred** (1926), which closed with a Technicolor reel depicting a gold-digger's fevered visions of her manifold sins embodied as infernal monsters (with costumes and masks designed by William Mortensen). They remade **Dante's Inferno** in 1935, with a variant plot and an even more impressive reconstruction of Hell.

FAUST – PRODUCTION PHOTOGRAPHS (*ABOVE, OPPOSITE &*
FOLLOWING PAGES).

FAUST

(F.W. Murnau, 1925-26: Germany)

The definitive cinematic version of the Faust legend, produced by UFA in Berlin.
Murnau illustrates this classic Satanic myth with suitably vivid and supernatural
scenes, including the horned and bat-winged Devil (played by Emil Janning) gliding
over gothic villages, arcane alchemical symbols, four apocalyptic riders galloping
through the sky, a gathering of the witches on Walpurgisnacht, and the words of an
unholy pact bursting into flaming hellfire. The whole film is beautifully shot in
chiaroscuro by cinematographer Carl Hoffmann, and remains one of the most
accomplished creations of the silent era. Although Murnau's film was clearly
impossible to better, and the story of Faust had already been filmed dozens of times,
yet more versions would emerge during the sound era; amongst these were a UK
production, **Faust Fantasy** (1935), and an Italian version, **La Leggenda Di Faust**
(1948). There were also early sound films of scenes from Charles Gounod's opera –
the 1929 Vitaphone short **Faust** featured tenor Charles Hackett in performance, and
the same company released **Giovanni Martinelli In The Prison Scene From Gounod's
"Faust"** the following year. The MGM production **Becky** (1927) also contained
scenes of a production of *Faust*, showing Tudor Williams as Mephistopheles, while
Universal's early horror classic **The Phantom Of The Opera** (1925) featured scenes
from a staging of *Faust* with Alexander Bevani as Mephistopheles. Mephistolean
"fancy dress" could be seen in a number of productions from this period, such as
Lasky's **Love 'Em And Leave 'Em** (1926) which starred Louise Brooks as a vamp
flapper.

"Fauſt"

The MAGICIAN
(Rex Ingram, 1925-26: USA)

Despite success with films such as **The Four Horsemen Of The Apocalypse** (1921), which made a star of Rudolph Valentino, director Ingram despised the Hollywood system and in 1924 decamped to the south of France. It was here that he made **The Magician**, his pinnacle work. Based on a novel by Somerset Maugham, the films deals with Haddo, an occultist (played by Paul Wegener) who has created a homunculus, an artificial creature, and requires blood from the heart of a virgin to imbue it with unholy life. He hypnotizes a young girl on the eve of her wedding and drags her to his bleak tower, where he has constructed an alchemical laboratory. Under his influence the girl has infernal hallucinations, including being ravished by a libidinal figure of Pan (played by the dancer/choreographer, Hubert Stowitts) at a witches' Sabbat. These erotic scenes of black magic are amongst the most effective in all silent cinema. Before the girl's heart can be hacked out and drained of blood, however, her fiancé intervenes; after a wild struggle, Haddo is burned alive and the tower is blown to smithereens. The occultist's dwarf servant – played by Henry Wilson, whose previous film roles included a pygmy and a baboon, both in episodes of Stoll Picture Productions' Sherlock Holmes series – ends up hanging from a branch, half-naked, and is attacked by a bat. A key Satanic-themed film in its own right, **The Magician** is also notable for being among the first in a small sub-genre of films inspired by the persona of Aleister Crowley, the British occultist once described as "the wickedest man in the world" after details emerged of orgies, blood sacrifices, devil-worship and sodomy at his Abbey of Thelema in Cefalu, Sicily. The creation of a homunculus, as seen in **The Magician**, is treated specifically in Crowley's 1917 novel *Moonchild*.

THE MAGICIAN – BLACK MAGIC ORGY; PRODUCTION PHOTOGRAPH.

MACISTE ALL'INFERNO – PRODUCTION PHOTOGRAPHS (*OPPOSITE PAGE, THIS PAGE*).

MACISTE ALL'INFERNO

("Maciste In Hell"; Guido Brignone, 1926: Italy)

This silent classic stands in its own right as one of the most astonishing cinematic visions of all time, with a sojourn in Hell more than equal to that created in **L'Inferno** of 1911; **Maciste All'Inferno** was in fact once described by acclaimed director Federico Fellini as one of the best ten films ever made. Lucia Zanussi plays Luciferina, the Devil's daughter, while Umberto Guarracino portrays the Horned One. The hero Maciste, as always, is played by strongman Bartolomeo Pagano. When Maciste is carnally tempted by Satan (here called Pluto), he ends up embattled in Hades, a zone of cannibalistic demons, infernal fiends and writhing, naked women (*risqué* scenes of female nudity were shown uncut at the Milan Fair, before censorship cuts were imposed).[1] Maciste's war against the demons includes decapitations, crushings and other brutal assaults, which are only intensified when the strongman is turned into a demon himself by Luciferina's carnal kiss. He is saved from eternal damnation by quelling a revolt led by the demon Barbariccia. The film's special effects by Segundo de Chómon include a mechanical dragon and claymation metamorphoses. Tortures and scenes of Pluto (played by Umberto Guarracino) devouring tiny victims alive recall similar atrocities from **L'Inferno**.[2] **Maciste All'Inferno** was produced by Societa Anonima Stefano Pittaluga.

1. Scenes from **Maciste All'Inferno** would be later used in at least two American exploitation films, **Maniac** (1934) and **Hell–A–Vision** (1936) – Brignone's original film was licensed for the USA by Olympia Macri Excelsior, who prepared a sound-enhanced version, **Maciste In Hell**, in 1931; lobby cards from its New York release by Capital Films show an apparent restoration of the nude scenes.

THE **SORROWS OF SATAN** – LYA DE PUTTI IN A BARE-
BREASTED SCENE FOR EUROPEAN RELEASE (*ABOVE*), AND
THE SHADOW OF SATAN (*RIGHT*); PRODUCTION
PHOTOGRAPHS.

The SORROWS OF SATAN
(D.W. Griffith, 1926: USA)
The already familiar story (based on the 1895 novel by Marie Corelli, and originally
filmed in England by G.B. Samuelson Productions in 1917) of a starving artist (in
this case, a novelist) who falls prey to the temptations of the Devil and agrees to
become his servant in exchange for riches. He is further held in thrall by a ravishing
princess (played by aristocratic arch-vamp Lya de Putti, who briefly appears with her
breast exposed in a scene cut from the US print), and marries her before discovering
she is secretly enamoured of Satan. Eventually he rejects his dark master, and ends
up back in the hovel he started in. Suave Adolphe Menjou plays Satan in human
guise, but His full bat-winged, bestial form is shown (by a clever use of shadows) at
the film's climax. This, allied to the skilful direction (in particular the opening scenes
of rebel angels being cast from Heaven) and the presence of the smouldering de Putti,
makes **The Sorrows Of Satan** perhaps the best Devil movie produced in the USA to
that date. Lya de Putti died from pneumonia in 1931, aged just thirty-four, following
an operation to remove a chicken bone from her oesophagus.

DER STUDENT VON PRAG – PRODUCTION PHOTOGRAPH.

Der STUDENT VON PRAG

("The Student Of Prague"; Henrik Galeen, 1926: Germany)
A remake of the 1913 film by Stellan Rye, with the director Henrik Galeen concentrating less on the occult and Faustian aspects of the story. The result is still extremely powerful, enhanced by the performances of Conrad Veidt as the student, and Werner Krauss as Scapinelli, the usurer and dealer in souls. Angular sets by Hermann Warm complete the ambience of expressionistic terror, making **Der Student Von Prag** and Galeen's version of **Alraune**, made a year later, the last major Weimar silent horror films. A third version of **Der Student Von Prag** was actually made in 1935, directed by Arthur Robison, and was the first with sound. It was also the only openly Satanic movie produced under the reign of Third Reich Cinema, and as such was allowed only limited distribution. Hanns Heinz Ewers, author of the original film – who was by then a proscribed figure in Nazi Germany – decried this version as illicit and sub-standard.

1. **Alraune** was almost immediately "remade" by Richard Oswald, whose sound version also featured the same star, Brigitte Helm.

THE MASKS OF THE DEVIL
(Victor Sjöström, 1928: USA)

In 1924 Swedish director Sjöström relocated to Hollywood where, under the name Victor Seastrom, he directed a series of films of which the most visually impressive was **The Masks Of The Devil** (1928); based on the 1910 novel *Die Masken Erwin Reiners* ("The Masks Of Erwin Reiner") by Jacob Wasserman, and borrowing from Oscar Wilde's *Picture Of Dorian Gray*, this opulent tale of the seduction of innocence was marked by sequences in which Reiner's mirror reflection grows increasingly Satanic, an effect achieved by diabolic double exposures.

SCHWARZE MESSE
("Black Mass"; Anonymous, 1928: Germany)

An 8-minute German stag reel, known in France as **Messe Noire**. The film depicts a coven of nude nuns being consecrated to Satan. This involves orgies, SM rites (including blood-letting) and lesbian scenes conducted by a masked high priest. **Les Mystères Du Couvent** ("Mysteries Of The Convent', also c.1928) was another underground blasphemo-porno film featuring nuns and monks engaged in various explicit sex acts, including lesbianism and sodomy; in the tradition of **Le Paysan Et La Nonne** ("The Peasant And The Nun") and **Le Moine** ("The Monk"), also from the 1920s. Germany's first porno-nun movie was probably **Klostergeheimnisse** ("Monastery Secrets", c.1912).

HELL'S BELLS
(Ub Iwerks, 1929: USA)

The fourth in Walt Disney's cartoon series **Silly Symphonies**, an early animated descent into Hell. Here we meet Satan himself, plus assorted demons, monsters and verminous creatures. The main featured music is Charles Gounod's *Marche Funèbre D'Une Marionnette* ("The Puppet's Funeral March", 1872-79), which later became famous as the theme tune for the long-running television show **Alfred Hitchcock Presents** (1955-62). Iwerks and Disney parted company in 1930, and Iwerks opened his own animation studio, backed by Disney's rival Pat Powers. **Hell's Fire** (1934), one of the Willie Whopper cartoons which he made from 1933-34, is a return visit to the Inferno featuring Satan on a throne of skulls, an array of rascals including Rasputin, Nero, Dr. Jekyll and Mr. Hyde, and Napoleon, and the twitching corpse of Prohibition (which Satan revives by pumping it full of liquor). Released that same year was the Betty Boop episode **Red Hot Mamma**, Betty's fiery nightmare of a trip into demon-infested Hell.

HELL'S FIRE – FRAME ENLARGEMENT.

SATURDAY'S LESSON
(Robert F. McGowan, 1929: USA)

Like many comedy franchises of the period, Hal Roach's **Our Gang** series included a number of comic-horror episodes; **Saturday's Lesson** featured frights from a man dressed as Satan, also a recurring figure in slapstick cinema. Other fright-oriented episodes included **Shivering Spooks** (1926, a play on the phoney spiritualist angle in which the gang uncover the fake séances of a grifter, who tries to scare them away by dressing as a ghost); **Spook Spoofing** (1927, playing on a black child's graveyard superstitions); and **Fast Freight** (1929, with a haunted house); while **Bouncing Babies** (1929) featured some grotesque Halloween costumes.

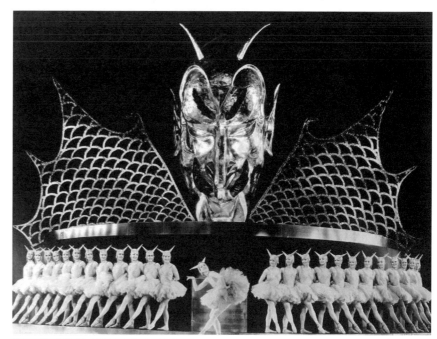

THE DEVIL'S CABARET – THE HADES BALLET; PRODUCTION PHOTOGRAPH.

The DEVIL'S CABARET
(Nick Grindé, 1930: USA)

A 17-minute, mildly risqué, 2-strip Technicolor Satanic musical from MGM, possibly constructed to accommodate footage from their abandoned, feature-length 2-strip Technicolor revue **The March Of Time** (1930). In **The Devil's Cabaret**, Satan (played by Charles Middleton) – whose secretary is a loose-breasted blonde in a "red-hot" mini-slip – bemoans his lack of "customers" and commands his lackey, Burns, to drum up business. Burns, after ordering six cases of bootleg liquor from "Scarface", decides to open a night-club which will lure sinners into Hades. The subterranean venue, with its huge backdrop of the Devil – from whose gaping mouth the guests arrive via a "tongue-slide" – serves illegal cocktails, is staffed by skimpy-costumed chorines, and features as its main act an exotic attraction billed as the "Hades Ballet". This sequence, taken from **The March Of Time**, is a stunning infernal dance number performed by the famous Albertina Rasch troupe in horned outfits, in front of a towering Satanic idol. Needless to say, the Devil's cabaret is a big hit. The 10-minute Warner Brothers short **The Devil's Parade** (also 1930) was another musical revue set in Hell, with Sidney Toler playing Satan. **Devilled Hams** (1937) and **Sin-copation** (1938) were short variations on the same theme. The concept of a Satanic musical set in Hell would realize its final fruition with the feature-length production **Hellazpoppin'**, released in 1941.

HELLBOUND TRAIN
(Eloyce Gist, 1930: USA)

The Hell-fearing religious tradition in black cinema traces back to **Hellbound Train**, a film by female evangelist Gist which depicted a series of brimstone-tinged morality plays – with each carriage of an infernal locomotive (driven by a swarthy horned Satan) representing a different sin – and was hugely popular in black churches, so much so that when an original copy was acquired by a US university, it had crumbled into hundreds of pieces through wear from multiple usage. Other aspects of the negro church were captured in documentary form in **We've Got The Devil On The Run** (1934), the filmed hellfire sermons and congregational songs of radio evangelist Lightfoot Solomon Michaux[1] in Washington DC.

1. Michaux was founder of the Radio Church of God, a pioneering religious movement disseminated through the airwaves, whose motto was "War Declared On The Devil!".

FÉTICHE – PRODUCTION PHOTOGRAPHS (*ABOVE, OPPOSITE &
OVERLEAF*).

FÉTICHE

("Fetish"; Wladyslaw Starewicz, 1933-34: France)

Also known by the title **Fétiche Mascotte** ("Fetish The Mascot"),[1] this is a 26-minute animated masterpiece by the subversive stop-motion pioneer Starewicz, a perverse mix of surrealistic grotesquerie, black humour and anthropomorphic animal adventures in Hell. Fetish, a toy dog, is brought to life by a child's teardrop, and embarks on a frenetic chase for an elusive orange – only to find that all roads lead to a demonic night-orgy hosted by Satan himself, and attended by skeletal, composite monsters that would appear to have influenced the work of Jan Svankmajer, as well as the animated horror films later produced by Tim Burton. Fetish would feature in four more short animated adventures: **Fétiche Prestidigitateur** ("Fetish The Magician", 1934), **Fétiche Se Marie** ("Fetish Gets Married", 1935) **Fétiche En Voyage De Noces** ("Fetish On Honeymoon", 1936), and **Fétiche Chez Les Sirènes** ("Fetish Among The Mermaids", 1937).

1. **Fétiche Mascotte**, which stands at around 600 metres in length, was actually edited down from its original length of 1000 metres (a version known only by the working code **L.S. 18**) by request of its distributors. In 1954, Starewicz used much of the cut footage to form a new film entitled **Gueule De Bois** ("Hangover"). A full reconstruction of **L.S. 18**, combining **Fétiche Mascotte**, **Gueule De Bois** and rushes from the Starewicz archive, was completed in 2012 under the title **Fétiche 33-12**, with a duration of some 38 minutes.

THE BLACK CAT – SATANIC MASS; PRODUCTION PHOTOGRAPH.

The BLACK CAT
(Edgar G. Ulmer, 1934: USA)

The second film in Universal's loose Edgar Allan Poe-inspired trilogy starring Bela Lugosi, in which they finally managed to pair him with Boris Karloff, thus placing their two horror icons in the same movie for the very first time. **The Black Cat** – released in England under the title **House Of Doom** – remains a seminal horror film for various reasons, the chemistry of its two stars just one aspect of a fascinating production. Although the script initially followed Poe's story more closely, this was virtually abandoned and replaced by a narrative that focuses on Satanism, necrophilia and sadism, engendering one of the most mesmeric and disturbing of all cinematic experiences. Karloff plays the architect Poelzig (named after the German occultist and architect Hans Poelzig), whose art-deco dreamhouse stands on the ruins of a fort destroyed in the war, and hundreds of corpses of the men that perished there; Lugosi plays the psychiatrist Werdegast, Poelzig's former associate, who has just been freed from a prison camp. On his way to take revenge on Poelzig, who he believes stole away his wife and daughter, Werdegast is involved in an accident with a newly-married couple; all three end up at Poelzig's mansion. Subsequent scenes include Werdegast, an aleurophobic, killing a black cat; Poelzig showing off a subterranean arcade where he keeps the bodies of numerous females suspended in glass coffins; and Poelzig, who is seen reading a book entitled *The Rites Of Lucifer*, conducting a black magic mass at which the new bride, still a virgin, is to be sacrificed. Finally, Werdegast achieves his revenge by skinning Poelzig alive with a scalpel, before being shot and detonating the whole mansion, burying himself, the Satanists and the glass-coffined brides forever. Ulmer's direction imbues the film with an oneiric atmosphere to match the weird convolutions of the narrative, which may have been inspired by the English sex magician Aleister Crowely and his notorious cult of Thelema, which had been based in Sicily during the 1920s, and reviled for the blood sacrifice of a black cat. With its compendium of barely sublimated psycho-sexual horrors and blasphemies, **The Black Cat** was the last classic of the pre-Hays Code enforcement period and a prime example of invoking Satan without showing scenes of Hell or the Devil Himself.

DANTE'S INFERNO – SCENE FROM HELL; PRODUCTION PHOTOGRAPH.

DANTE'S INFERNO
(Harry Lachmann, 1935: USA)

Based on Fox's 1924 **Dante's Inferno**, but changing its villain from slum landlord to corrupt carnival owner, Lachmann's remake is really only notable for its staggering vision of Hell, based on engravings by Gustave Doré. Although reduced to some eight minutes in length, this painterly sequence – designed by art director Willy Pogany, set designer Ben Carré, and special effects director Fred Sersen, and photographed by Rudolf Maté – supersedes all others with its sweeping infernal panoramas, pain labyrinths ablaze with fire and brimstone, and convolutions of writhing, semi-naked sinners in eternal damnation and torment (said to have been choreographed by

DANTE'S INFERNO – SCENES FROM HELL; PRODUCTION
PHOTOGRAPHS (*ABOVE, OPPOSITE & FOLLOWING PAGES*).

Hubert Stowitts, the priapic faun from Rex Ingram's **The Magician**). Dwarf actors
Angelo Rossitto and John George are also said to feature, uncredited, in the film,
whose central attraction may have been inspired by Hell Gate, a legendary ride from
the heyday of Coney Island's Dreamland funfair.

PLUTO'S JUDGEMENT DAY
(David Hand, 1935: USA)

One of the first Mickey Mouse cartoons shot in Technicolor, and the last to flirt with "horrific" imagery. A spectral cat lures Mickey's dog, Pluto, through the fanged rictus of a huge feline statue, and down into the bowels of Hell to be judged for his crimes against pussycats. A judge, jury and Satanic prosecutor – all cats – hear testimony from his physically and psychologically shattered victims, before sentencing him to burn alive. As in Dave Fleischer's **Red Hot Mamma** from the previous year, it turns out to be a nightmare caused by sleeping too near to the fire.[1] **Pluto's Judgement Day** features outstanding drawing and animation, including extreme close-ups and perspectives, in depicting the inferno and especially the luridly demonic figure of Pluto's chief tormentor (voiced by Billy Bletcher).

1. Elements of both **Pluto's Judgement Day** and **Red Hot Mamma** can be found in the later Famous Studios **Noveltoon** entry **Mutt In A Rut** (1949), one of just two cartoons featuring a bad-tempered hound named Dog Face (the first was 1945's **A Self-Made Mongrel**). In a fire-heated nightmare, kitten-hater Dog Face is tortured in Hell and is finally cooked on a griddle by a huge feline burger-flipper.

HELL-A-VISION – PRODUCTION PHOTOGRAPH.

HELL-A-VISION
(Louis Sonney, 1936: USA)

A real oddity from exploitation master Sonney, comprised of "true crime" clips from the **March Of Crime** series (including John Dillinger), old scenes of Hell from the 1926 film **Maciste All'Inferno**, and other footage which includes female nudity. These are supposed to be deviant image signals from the underworld, picked up by a scientist's "thought relativity machine". This patchwork method of film assembly was reflected in publicity stills for the movie, which were made from image collages. Sonney may have been inspired by **Uncle Si And The Sirens**, an 8-minute Cine Art home projection reel made around 1930, and often used as a support film in roadshow programs. It tells the tale of a yokel farmer who constructs his own television set and is soon picking up mysterious transmissions of dancing girls and naked temptresses.

SUNDAY GO TO MEETIN' TIME
(Friz Freleng, 1936: USA)

An entry in Leon Schlesinger's full-colour **Merrie Melodies** series, featuring several popular songs of the time, **Sunday Go To Meetin' Time** is minor classic of Satanic visions. Nicodemus, a stereotypical "coon", is up to his usual tricks – dodging church, shooting dice, and stealing chickens – when he gets knocked unconscious and has a vivid dream of being sent to Hell for his sins. Here he is brought before Satan – a towering, horned figure in red – scorched by flames, used as a human pinball, and tormented by demonic imps with pitchforks. Seeing the error of his ways, Nicodemus rushes to church and finds redemption in an uplifting finale. Satan's fall from a terrifying icon of the silent cinema to a haunter of animated comics was symptomatic of an increasingly sterile and repressive cultural climate, one which would not be liberated again until the permissive 1960s enabled a cinematic rebirth in the form of Roman Polanski's **Rosemary's Baby** and the many Luciferian horrors that followed.

INDEX of FILMS

Gareth Hugh Janus is editor of numerous books on pulp cinema and pulp art. His main project is the popular book series **VOLUPTUOUS TERRORS**, an ongoing collection showcasing classic Italian horror and exploitation film posters of the 1950s to 1980s.

VOLUPTUOUS TERRORS – THE SERIES TO DATE

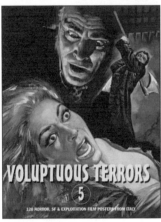

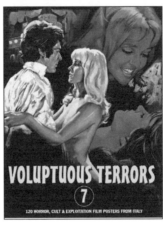
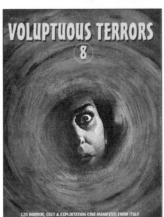

SHADOWS IN A PHANTOM EYE – THE SERIES TO DATE